Schiffer Publishing Ltd

Solid-Colored Dinnerware
Depression and Mid-Century

Mark Gonzalez

4880 Lower Valley Road Atglen, Pennsylvania 19310

Dedication

For Randy, Mistie, and Emmie.

Other Schiffer Books by Mark Gonzalez:
Taylor, Smith and Taylor China Company, 0-7643-2071-8, $29.95

Other Schiffer Books on Related Subjects
Schiffer Publishing has a wide variety of books featuring the best in pottery, ceramic and tile wares. Please visit our website at www.schifferbooks.com for more information.

Copyright © 2008 by Mark Gonzalez
Library of Congress Control Number: 2007940151

Designed by John P. Cheek
Cover design by Bruce Waters
Type set in New Baskerville BT/Zurich BT

ISBN: 978-0-7643-2846-6
Printed in China

Schiffer Books are available at special discounts for bulk purchases for sales promotions or premiums. Special editions, including personalized covers, corporate imprints, and excerpts can be created in large quantities for special needs. For more information contact the publisher:

Published by Schiffer Publishing Ltd.
4880 Lower Valley Road
Atglen, PA 19310
Phone: (610) 593-1777; Fax: (610) 593-2002
E-mail: Info@schifferbooks.com

For the largest selection of fine reference books on this and related subjects, please visit our web site at **www.schifferbooks.com**
We are always looking for people to write books on new and related subjects. If you have an idea for a book please contact us at the above address.

This book may be purchased from the publisher.
Include $3.95 for shipping.
Please try your bookstore first.
You may write for a free catalog.

In Europe, Schiffer books are distributed by
Bushwood Books
6 Marksbury Ave.
Kew Gardens
Surrey TW9 4JF England
Phone: 44 (0) 20 8392-8585; Fax: 44 (0) 20 8392-9876
E-mail: info@bushwoodbooks.co.uk
Website: www.bushwoodbooks.co.uk
Free postage in the U.K., Europe; air mail at cost.

Contents

Chapter One

Introduction

The practice of making solid colored dinnerware starts in the 1920s. Most collectors agree it was the popularity of Depression glass that steered potteries in the direction of colored glazes. Wares made up to the mid-1920s were white ware with a clear glaze, but by the late 1920s, many potteries started using the colors from Depression glass such as pink, green, yellow, and to a lesser degree, rust. Ivory glazes were also developed during this time.

Towards the late 1930s, the older Depression glazes were replaced by one of two sets of colors. The bold Fiesta-type colors (red, cobalt, yellow, green, maroon, turquoise) and the pastel glazes were highly favored by consumers. The Fiesta-type glazes remained popular until the late 1940s when they were replaced by darker, more modern colors; forest green, chartreuse, gray, burgundy, and brown. Pastel glazes continued to be popular and by the 1950s companies were making speckled glazes.

By the 1960s, American potteries started closing down. Imports of "Fine China" and indestructible Melmac and other plastic dinnerware put an end to many companies, and, as a result, American made solid colored dinnerware. What we are left with is a wide array of shapes in dozens of colors made over a period of approximately five decades.

This book features just some of the collectible solid colored dinnerware lines, namely Fiesta and Lu-Ray along with many other lines which are often confused with one another. While many potteries would commonly mark their dinnerware, when it comes to the colorware, especially pieces from the late 1930s to the late 1940s, most, but not all, did not receive a backstamp.

I would like to acknowledge the following people for submitting photos. Their help and willingness to share is greatly appreciated.

Dominick Abel and Kathleen Moloney, Candy Fagerlin, Lillian King, Lori Lipkin, Fred Mutchler, Terri Puleo, Larisa Self, Fran and Carl Stone, and Eva Zia

Chapter Two

Atlas-Globe China Company
Cambridge, Ohio (1926 - 1932)

Atlas-Globe was in operation for a very short time. They produced semi-porcelain dinnerware Broadway and Old Holland. Atlas-Globe was reorganized and became the Oxford Pottery Company and eventually Universal Potteries. You may find Atlas-Globe shapes with Universal backstamps.

Old Holland was made in plain with decals and in two-tone contrasting colors. It dates from the early 1930s and may or may not be marked.

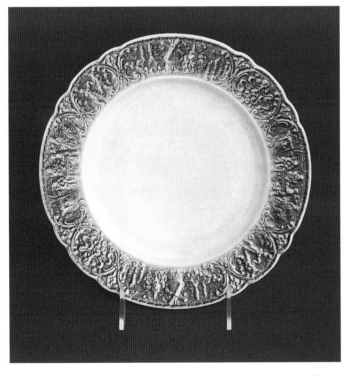

Old Holland 9" plate in yellow with brown wash trim, $6-8.

Chapter Three

Cronin China Company
Minerva, Ohio (1928 - 1956)

Cronin China made semi-porcelain dinnerware and kitchenware. The only solid colored dinnerware line was Zephyr, but the glazes can also be found on their Bake Oven kitchenware. In their later years, Cronin produced several kitchenware lines including Tulip in pastel blue with cobalt tulips, pink with cobalt tulips, and yellow with brown tulips. They also made kitchenware in contrasting color combinations such as bases in pink with black lids. Several Cronin Bake Oven pieces have been found with the Sevilla mark. See section on Sevilla for more.

Cronin blue jug, late 1940s, $8-10.

Cronin Tulip covered dish, $6-8.

Zephyr

Zephyr was Cronin China's ring shape from the late 1930s. In solid colored glazes, it was marketed under several different names. In one case it was called Hollywood Colors and sold in an ensemble set with the following glazes; Wiltshire Yellow, Avalon Blue, Sycamore Brown, La Brea Burgundy, Pico Turquoise, Catalina Green, Beverly Blue, and Pasadena Rose. It was also sold as Mardi Gras and Luciente.

Most pieces will be unmarked. Because of a lack of backstamp, it is often confused with Homer Laughlin's Fiesta and Harlequin. Most decaled Zephyr will have a Cronin backstamp.

Zephyr 9" and 7" plates. 9" plate, $5-7, 7" plate, $4-6.

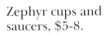
Zephyr cups and saucers, $5-8.

Zephyr creamer and sugar, restyled version. Creamer, $3-4; sugar, $7-9

Zephyr covered sugars.
Left, the Restyled version; the
original angled version is on the
right. $7-9

Zephyr fruit cups in yellow,
green, and red. $1-2.

Cronin pie plate. These have been
found in four Zephyr colors; red,
cobalt, green, and yellow. Because
they are unmarked, they are almost
always mistakenly identified as Harlequin by Homer Laughlin. $8-10

Tab handled plate.
There are at least two sizes of tab
plates and they have been found
in green and burgundy. $8-10.

Chapter Four
French-Saxon China Company
Sebring, Ohio (1911 - 1964)

French-Saxon made several lines of colorware. The Zephyr shape was used for Romany and Ranchero. Their plain round coupe shape Aloha was made in chartreuse, dark green, burgundy, and rust. The Aloha Pastel line used many of the same shapes in pastel shades. One ad gave names to the four pastel colors; warm pink, turquoise green, Delft blue, and canary yellow. The Aloha shape had tilted bodies with angular handles, but the later pastel version had more conventional shapes that would go on to be used by Royal China — the company that bought French-Saxon in 1964.

Aloha dinner plate and teacup in gray. Plate, $6-8; teacup, $4-6.

Romany & Ranchero

Romany & Ranchero were both based on the Zephyr shape, but have different color assortments. Romany, which was often sold as Granada by some retailers, was offered in cobalt, red, yellow and green during the late 1930s and early 1940s. Sometimes sets are found with turquoise instead of green. Ranchero, from the late 1940s, came in gray, maroon, dark green, and chartreuse.

Besides the solid colors, Zephyr was also offered with decal treatments for its entire production run.

Many times Ranchero and Romany are marked with special backstamps with their respective names.

Romany place settings in turquoise, red, cobalt, and yellow. *Courtesy of Eva Zia.*

Romany cups and saucers in red, cobalt, green, and yellow. $5-8. *Courtesy of Eva Zia.*

Ranchero 9" plates in chartreuse and burgundy. Romany 7" plate in red. 9" plates, $5-7; 7", $4-6.

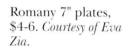

Romany 7" plates, $4-6. *Courtesy of Eva Zia.*

Ranchero burgundy and gray plates, $5-8.

Cups and saucers in gray, yellow, and dark green, $5-8.

Romany sugar in turquoise and creamer in red. Sugar, $7-9, creamer, $3-4. *Courtesy of Eva Zia.*

Ranchero salt and pepper shakers in burgundy and yellow, $8-10 pr.

Formal style French-Saxon shakers often found in sets of Ranchero, $8-10 pr. *Courtesy of Eva Zia.*

Covered vegetable in yellow, $12-15. *Courtesy of Eva Zia.*

Ranchero chop plate in dark green, $6-8. *Courtesy of Eva Zia.*

11

Chapter Five

W.S. George Pottery Company
East Palestine, Ohio (1898 - 1960)

W.S. George is named for its founder, William S. George. Though the main offices of W.S. George were in East Palestine, in 1931 there were at least four production plants. Two were in East Palestine, Ohio (Plants 1 and 4), one in Canonsburg, Pennsylvania (Plant 2), and the fourth in Kittanning, Pennsylvania (Plant 3).

W.S. George produced hotel and toilet wares, and dinnerware — both in solid colors and with decals. Some of their more collectible lines are Basketweave, Elmhurst Pastels, Georgette, Geometric, Bolero, Rainbow, and Petit Point. You may find many W.S. George pieces with the Cavitt-Shaw backstamp — a distributor for W.S. George.

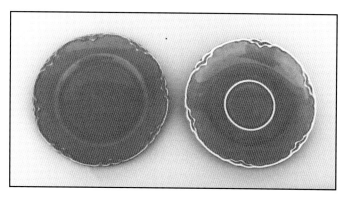

Raddison 6" plate and saucer in pink, $1-2.

Raddison baker in green, $4-5.

Georgex teapot in turquoise, $20-25.

Georgex teapot in medium blue, $20-25

W. S. George's Vesta Alba shape from the late 1930s.

Basketweave

Basketweave was made throughout the 1930s and is among the easiest of the W.S. George shapes to find from that decade. It was created as a round shape with basketweave embossing around the rim, hence its name. It was initially offered in single color sets of either Blue Bonnet, Gretna Green, or Maple Bisque. Brown was added later. There are many treatments that combine solid color Basketweave along with decals.

The only downside to collecting Basketweave, or other lines from the early 1930s, is the high amount of crazing and discoloration. It wasn't until the late 1930s and early 1940s that potteries perfected their colored glazes.

Basketweave covered dish in green, $12-15.

Basketweave small platter in brown, $4-5

Bolero

First produced in the mid-1930s, Bolero is commonly found with decals. In some cases, pieces can be found in solid colored glazes; alabaster, lemon yellow, turquoise, cobalt and brown.

Bolero covered sugar in yellow, fruit cup and 6" plate in rust. Sugar, $8-10; fruit cup, $2-3; 6" plate, $2-3.

Elmhurst

Elmhurst was produced in the late 1930s. It's a fluted shape with formal handles and finials. This dramatic line must not have sold terribly well since its difficult to find today. In1939 trade journal ad, Elmhurst in colored glazes was described as, "...the result of long research and experimentation at the big potteries of the W.S. George Company. Plain bright colors were first obtained and used in the pottery field, but it remained for the W.S. George Pottery to perfect and stabilize the soft hues of pastel tints now available on the Elmhurst shape."

It was offered in the solid colors, Blue, Pink, Yellow, Apple Green, Maple Sugar, and Turquoise as Elmhurst Pastels. No doubt this was to compete with the successful Lu-Ray Pastels by Taylor Smith & Taylor.

Besides the pastel glazes, Elmhurst can be found in ivory with decals. Most pieces are marked with the general W.S. George backstamp with the Elmhurst name.

Elmhurst marking.

Elmhurst covered casserole in turquoise, $20-25. *Courtesy of Stephanie Croquez.*

Elmhurst creamer in yellow and covered sugar in pink Creamer, $3-4; sugar, $7-9. *Courtesy of Stephanie Croquez.*

Elmhurst vegetable bowl in turquoise, $5-7. *Courtesy of Stephanie Croquez.*

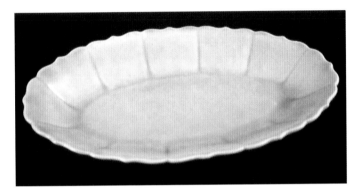

Elmhurst sauceboat stand in pink, $6-8.
Courtesy of Stephanie Croquez.

Elmhurst pickle in turquoise, $6-8.
Courtesy of Stephanie Croquez.

Elmhurst place setting. *Courtesy of Stephanie Croquez.*

1950s W.S. George cups and saucers in burgundy, yellow, gray, and dark green. $5-8.

Fifties Lines

In the 1950s, W. S. George offered several lines of solid colored dinnerware using plain round coupe shape flatware and a mix of hollowware. Some of the hollowware came from an old formal style Deerwood shape while others came from the more modern and casual Ranchero shape. At least three different types of glazes were used in the 1950s; bold solid colors of maroon, chartreuse, dark green, and gray, the pastel colors yellow, pink, chartreuse, and gray, and the speckled glazes green, pink, yellow, gray, blue, and brown.

Most of these wares are not marked, but some will have a general W.S. George marking or the Cavitt-Shaw backstamp. Many dinnerware sets from this time mixed and matched solid glazes with decals. Also covered pieces such as casseroles and sugars are often found with their bases in a solid color and the lid with a decal treatment. In some cases, speckled 1950s W.S. George ware will be marked, "Festive."

1950s W.S. George 9" plates, $5-7.

1950s W.S. George creamer, covered sugar, and sauceboat. Creamer, $3-4; sugar, $7-9, and sauceboat, $8-10.

Ranchero creamer, fruit cup, teacup, and saucer in speckled green glazes.

1950s pastel speckled glazes gray, pink, green, and yellow.

1950s speckled glazes gray sauceboat and yellow creamer. Sauceboat, $8-10; creamer, $3-4.

Geometric

Geometric was offered by W.S. George in the early 1930s, and was similar to Basketweave in many respects. They both were sold in single color sets, glazed in white with decals, and had under glaze border treatments along the embossing. Unlike Basketweave, however, Geometric didn't sell very well.

In almost every case, Geometric is found in what vintage ads describe as an, "Early American Blue Glaze." Pieces that are marked bear the general W.S. George backstamp along with the shape's name.

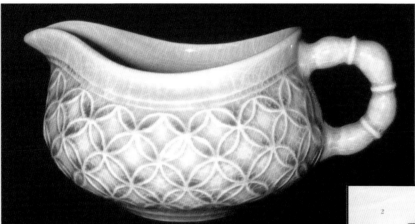

Geometric Creamer, $3-4. *Courtesy of Terri Puleo.*

GEOMETRIC BLUE GLAZED WARE, W. S. George Pottery Co.'s, East Palestine, O., latest offering to the trade. In this era of color, the blue glaze, a color for which there has been an incessant demand for some time, provides a delightful shade of coloring, as well as a unique and artistic shape, as the illustration above testifies. The embossing is of a nature that produces by its high lights a very pleasing two tone effect. Shown in New York by S. H. Slobodkin, 20 West 23rd St.

Georgette

Georgette, a.k.a. Petal, is by far the most available and popular of the W.S. George solid color lines. The round scalloped shape was made in colors from the late 1930s to early 40s, medium blue, green, rose, and yellow, as well as colors from the late 1940s and early 1950s; dark green, maroon, chartreuse, and gray.

Shakers were not made for Georgette. Instead, they were picked up from the already existing Elmhurst line.

Georgette is rarely marked and is often confused with Mt. Clemens' Toulon shape.

Petal flatware.
Courtesy of Lori Lipkin.

Petal soup bowls, $4-6.

Petal platters in dark green and pink, $6-8.

Petal platter in pink and baker in gray, $6-8.

Petal in burgundy and pink.

Petal sauceboat in green, $8-10

These shakers are used with several W.S. George lines and can be found in the Petal and Elmhurst glazes, $8-10 pr.

Petal teapot in green, $30-35. *Courtesy of Terri Puleo.*

Rainbow

Rainbow was first offered by W.S. George in the mid-1930s. It came in several solid colored glazes as well as white with decals. It is distinguished by its scalloped edge and very narrow rim. The cover for the sugar bowl was made to interchange with the creamer. Pink and green are somewhat easy to find followed by blue, yellow, and tan.

Rainbow double eggcup, $10-12

Below:
Rainbow covered sugar and creamer. Sugar, $7-9, creamer, $3-4.

Rainbow: Petit-Point

Petit-Point is made up of the Rainbow shapes, but has an embossed floral petit-point design covering the entire piece. It was made in dark blue, green, yellow, and tan. It is doubtful Petit-Point will be found with decals since the embossed bodies are not suited for them.

Rainbow and Petit-Point are usually marked with their respective shape names.

Petit-Point 9" plate, $5-7.

Chapter Six
Edwin M. Knowles China Company
Newell, West Virginia (1900 - 1963)

Knowles large jardinière. These have been found in green and pink colors, $250+

Knowles large jardinière, back.

Just like many other potteries of the early twentieth century, Knowles made toilet ware, hotel ware and dinnerware, however the toilet ware and other specialties were phased out by the 1920s. The most collected lines from Knowles are Yorktown and Esquire. The Tia Juana treatment, a Mexican-theme decal which appeared on several Knowles shapes, and the fruit pattern are also collectible.

Knolwes promotional charger in pink. UND

Creamlace shape platter in green, $8-10.

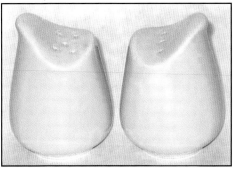

Criterion shape shakers from the 1950s, $8-10 pr.

Left: Bread tray in pastel blue. These were made in the late 1940s to the early 1950s in pastel glazes. $6-8.

Accent

Accent was produced primarily in the 1950s, and became Knowles' standard coupe shape for most of the decade. The coffeepot and shakers are the only items not designed specifically for Accent. They were picked up from the Potomac shape.

Accent can be found in several forms; decals, pastel glazes, 50s colors of dark green, gray, chartreuse and brown, and in solid white. The 50s colors and solid white were sold through Montgomery Wards. Wards sold some accessory pieces with their solid color accent line including a tid-bit tray and snack set.

Accent will generally be marked with the square Knowles backstamp, although the pastel line may sometimes be marked, "Sunset Glazes."

Accent creamer in chartreuse and covered sugar in dark green. Creamer, $2-3, sugar, $3-4.

Accent lug soups and fruit cups in brown, dark green, gray, and chartreuse. $2-3.

Accent cups and saucers in brown, dark green, gray, and chartreuse. $1-2.

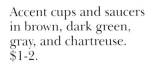

Accent serving bowl in brown, $6-8.

Accent snack tray and teacup in chartreuse, $6-8.

Sunset Glazes 10" plate in pink, $2-3.

Sunset Glazes backstamp. This must have been used in the late 1950s or early 1960s since the marking guarantees the ware to be detergent proof. This was not typical of backstamps prior to the late 1950s.

Accent teacups and saucers in the pastel glazes, $1-2.

Sunset Glazes sugar and creamer.
These were picked up from the Potomac shape. Sugar, $3-4, and the creamer, $2-3.

Shakers in dark green.
The shakers were picked up from the Potomac shape and sold with Accent, $6-8.

Creme Flute

Creme Flute was made in the 1930s until the 1950s with decals, but it can also be found in pastel glazes. Such Creme Flute is usually not marked.

Creme Flute in pastel glazes. Teacup and saucer, $3-4; plates, $5-6.

Cameo

Cameo is an early 1930s line. It was given a heavily embossed rim which was typical of many dinnerware lines of the day. Cameo is not uncommon in green or yellow (with and without decals) and may also be found in pink. It is usually marked with a simple Knowles backstamp along with the shape name.

Creme Flute sugar in blue, $8-10.

Cameo platter in Depression green, $6-8.

Deanna

Deanna was a ring shape first made by Knowles in 1938. There are three light rings at the rim of flatware and on the bases of hollowware. It was made in solid colors, white with decals, and in a tan body. The solid colors include; maroon, red, blue, yellow, green, pink, brown, pastel blue, pastel yellow, and peach.

By the 1950s, the older solid colored lines such as Deanna and Yorktown were replaced by more modern Accent and Potomac shapes.

The Deanna flatware, shakers, eggcup were used in the Aladdin and Beverly shapes. Once in a while, Beverly hollowware with Deanna flatware can be found in pastel glazes.

Most pieces of Deanna have the generic Knowles backstamp.

Deanna teapot in pink, sugar in blue, and the creamer in yellow. Teapot $35-40, creamer, $5-6, and sugar, $6-8. *Courtesy of Terri Puleo.*

Deanna flatware in pink, burgundy, green, yellow, and pastel blue.

Deanna serving bowl in turquoise, $5-6.

Deanna creamer in red and covered sugar in pink. Creamer, $5-6; sugar $6-8.

Right: Knowles ashtray in red. These ashtrays have been found in all the Deanna and Yorktown colors. They usually have the generic Knowles backstamp and were probably sold with both lines. $8-10.

Deanna coaster with decal promoting the 1939 New York World Fair decal, $6-8.

Deanna sugar marked with a worn, over-the-glaze stamp: "El Rio" ware, East Liverpool, Ohio. $6-8.

Marion Childs' dish in pink, $12-15

Marion

Marion was a fluted shape from the 1930s. It has been found in the three standard Depression glazes, pink, green and yellow. Many times the yellow glazed pieces have decals.

As with Cameo, which was produced around the same time, Marion is marked with a simple Knowles backstamp and the shape name.

Maryland

The Maryland shape was introduced in the very late 1920s. It was produced in three Depression era glazes, pink, yellow and green, or, as Knowles called them, Old Rose, Roma, and Nile. As most potteries did in the late 1920s to early 1930s, Knowles offered Maryland in single-color sets.

Maryland can be identified by its scalloped shape and paneled rim. Every other panel features embossed roses. The shape can also be found in ivory and the light yellow glaze with decals.

Alice Ann, an octagonal shape from the 1930s, can also be found in the three Depression era glazes.

Old Rose teapot, $35-40.

Old Rose (Maryland shape) 7" plate. The red plate in the background is from Knowles' Williamsburg shape. Maryland plate, $3-5; Williamsburg plate, $6-8.

Roma (Maryland shape) coupe soup with decals, $5-7.

27

Plaid

Plaid was offered in the late 1930s in both solid colors and white with decals. When in solid colors, it was often sold as, "Highlight Plaid" which was an appropriate name since the colored glazes brought out the plaid embossing. Vintage ads describe Highlight Plaid as, "…distinctive embossed design is the result of the contrast between the deeper tone taken by the glaze in the depressed areas and the highlights on the raised portions of the pattern."

Highlight Plaid was offered in single color sets of yellow, blue and green. It is usually marked with the general Knowles backstamp.

Plaid oval platter, $6-8.

Plaid creamer and sugar, sans lid. Creamer, $3-4; sugar, $7-9. *Courtesy of Terri Puleo.*

Potomac

Potomac was a rim shape offered during the 1940s and 1950s. The Accent shape used the Potomac coffeepot and shakers. As a result, those pieces can be found in the pastel and 50s colors used in the Accent line.

Other Potomac pieces, namely flatware, were made in the 50s Accent colors, brown, gray, dark green, and chartreuse. Such pieces are almost always unmarked.

Potomac 9" plates in dark green, gray, and brown, $5-7.

Utility Ware

Knowles offered its oven proof Utility Ware in the late 1930s and 1940s in solid colored glazes in with decals. The simple round shape was crafted with concentric rings towards the base. Most pieces are marked with a Utility Ware backstamp.

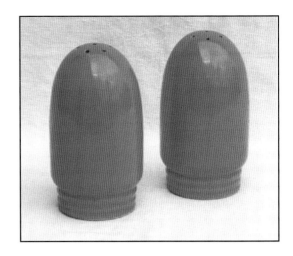

Utility Ware range shakers in red, $12-15 pr.

Utility Ware 9" plate in red, $8-10.

Utility Ware covered leftover dishes with fruit decals, $8-10.

Utility Ware covered jug in red, $20-25. *Courtesy of Eva Zia.*

KNOWLES UTILITY WARE

NEW YORK HOUSEWARES SHOW
PENNSYLVANIA HOTEL—JULY 10-16
CHICAGO FURNITURE SHOW—JULY 5-16

A complete line of cooking, serving refrigerator and kitchenware in seven beautiful color combinations. Modern colorful and practical in every detail

Yorktown

Yorktown was made in the late 1930s as a ring shape with sundial finials and sweeping tab handles. It was used for both solid colors and decals until the late 1940s. It is often marked with a special Yorktown backstamp.

This is one of the few dinnerware lines to have candle holders. Usually, these were not standard items in a line of dinnerware. Besides Knowles' Yorktown, HLC's Fiesta and Harlequin, TST's Plymouth, and Paden City's Caliente all had candle holders.

Yorktown flatware in blue, yellow, red, and rust.

Yorktown promotional coaster, $10-12.

Yorktown teacup and saucer in burgundy, $7-10.

Yorktown shakers in a true red glaze, $12-15 pr.

Yorktown shakers in ivory. The ivory creamer is from Knowles' Arcadia shape.

Yorktown covered sugar in green and covered casserole in yellow. Sugar, $12-15; casserole, $35-45.

Yorktown creamer in blue and covered sugar in yellow. Creamer, $8-10; sugar, 12-15.

Yorktown console bowl, $18-20.

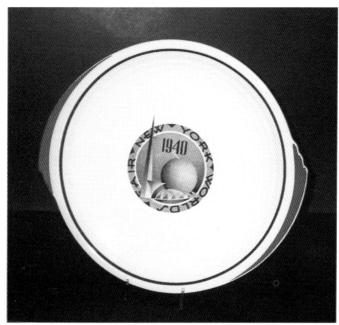

Yorktown chop plate with a
1940 New York World's Fair
decal. $10-12 solid color. With
World's Fair decal, $45-50.

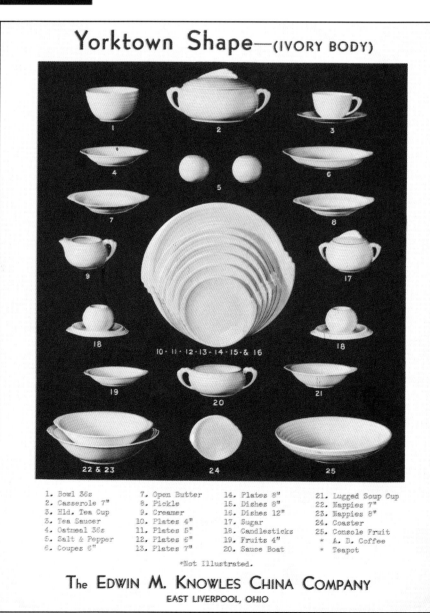

Yorktown Shape—(IVORY BODY)

1. Bowl 36s	7. Open Butter	14. Plates 8"	21. Lugged Soup Cup
2. Casserole 7"	8. Pickle	15. Dishes 8"	22. Nappies 7"
3. Hld. Tea Cup	9. Creamer	16. Dishes 12"	23. Nappies 8"
3. Tea Saucer	10. Plates 4"	17. Sugar	24. Coaster
4. Oatmeal 36s	11. Plates 5"	18. Candlesticks	25. Console Fruit
5. Salt & Pepper	12. Plates 6"	19. Fruits 4"	* A. D. Coffee
6. Coupes 6"	13. Plates 7"	20. Sauce Boat	* Teapot

*Not Illustrated.

The EDWIN M. KNOWLES CHINA COMPANY
EAST LIVERPOOL, OHIO

Chapter Seven

Knowles Taylor & Knowles
East Liverpool, Ohio (1872-1929)

Knowles Taylor & Knowles, or KTK, is well known for making the light weight porcelain, Lotus Ware. They also made semi-vitreous dinnerware. Two such lines were Victory and the paneled shape Gloria.

Knowles Taylor & Knowles vase, $10-15.

Vase marking.

"Lotus"

"Lotus" is the name given to this ware by pottery author Harvey Duke. The shape is a semi-porcelain version of the lightweight Lotus ware made by Knowles Taylor & Knowles, hence the name.

It was made during the very early 1930s in Depression glazes. At least five have been found thus far; blue, rust, pink, green, and yellow with pink and green being the most common.

Unfortunately, Lotus is often found crazed and discolored.

"Lotus" platter. The batter jug is in a similar Depression green glaze. It was made by C.C. Thompson Pottery of East Liverpool, Ohio. Platter, $6-8; Thompson jug, $6-8.

"Lotus" 9-inch plate and soup bowl in pink. Plate, $5-7; bowl, $4-6.

"Lotus" 36s bowl and 7-inch plate. Bowl, $6-8; plate $3-4.

"Lotus" platter and fruit cup in pink. Platter, $6-8; fruit cup, $1-2.

Chapter Eight

Homer Laughlin China Company
Newell, West Virginia (1871 - present)

Founded by brothers Homer and Shakespeare Laughlin, the company started out in East Liverpool, Ohio and expaned to Newell, West Virginia. By 1929, the East Liverpool plants closed. Homer Laughlin is still in operation today in Newell.

Homer Laughlin has made just about every type of ware in its long history including specialties, hotel ware, dinnerware and art china. From 1928 until 1942,

Frederick Rhead was art director. During this time some of HLC most collected wares were made such as Fiesta, Harlequin, Virginia Rose, Riviera, Century, and OvenServe.

Since 1986, HLC has been producing the Fiesta line with new colors and additional contemporary shapes. They continue to make wares for retailers as well as restaurants and hotels.

An assortment of Homer Laughlin shapes.

Betty Crocker bowls in turquoise and yellow, $20-25.

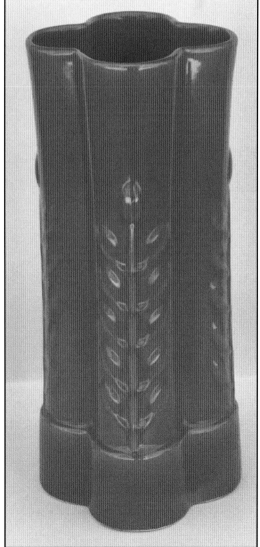
Frederick Rhead "Four-tube" vase. UND

Apple Tree bowls in pumpkin, melon yellow and turquoise. *Courtesy of Candy Fagerlin.*

Promotional casserole and pie plate for Royal Metal in Fiesta red, $35-50.

Shell plate in Fiesta red, $200+

Beer stein in Leaf Green marked with a Wells Art Glazes backstamp. The deco tumbler has an incised HLC marking. Both from the early 1930s. UND

Leaf saucer in green made for Kraft Cheese products, $250+

Drawings for proposed solid-colored dishes from the late 1930s.

Deco ashtrays in pumpkin, rust, and rose, $85-95. These are generic-shaped ashtrays that have been found in the glazes mentioned, as well as melon yellow and ivory. Sometimes they will have the Wells Art Glazes or OvenServe backstamps. They were first made in 1931.

Handled bread tray in rose, circa 1933. $200+

Potters plates made for the 1939-1940 New York World's Fair, $20-25.

World's Fair potter plate in turquoise, $20-25.

An assortment of World's Fair items.

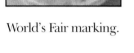

Small World's Fair vases.

FDR mug. UND

Below:
Tea Rose shape cup and saucer in ivory and yellow. The Tea Rose shape was a special breakfast set shape made for Quaker Oats in the 1930s. It is most often found with decals. UND in solid colors.

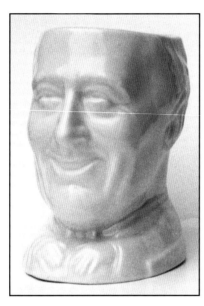

Divided bakers in rose and chartreuse, $35-40.

Spoon rests from the 1950s. These have been found in Harlequin yellow, dark green (shown), turquoise, red, and medium green. Spoon rests with decals or the under glaze Dura Print decorations are not hard to find. $150-185.

Before Fiesta was reintroduced in 1986, HLC toyed with the idea of making Russell Wright Casual China. Shown are some of the RW pieces made at HLC in the mid-1980s. UND

Left: Divided bakers in turquoise and yellow from the 1950s, $35-40.

Antique Orleans

The decal shape, Orleans, was made from 1931 until the mid-1940s. It has been found in at least three Wells Art glazes; rust, green, and rose. Undecorated ivory blanks can also be found.

The solid colors must have been made early since they are found in single color sets typical of the Depression era. Most decaled Orleans is marked with a general HLC backstamp and date code, but Antique Orleans is marked with a special "Antique Orleans" marking with no mention of Homer Laughlin or dates.

The sugar for Orleans was originally made as an open piece, but in 1936, a second version was made complete with a lid.

Antique Orleans markings.

Antique Orleans 9" plate in rose and cup and saucer in rust. Plate, $7-9; the cup and saucer, $8-11.

Antique Orleans platter in Leaf Green, $10-12.

Antique Orleans 9" plate in rose, $7-9.

Antique Orleans platter in rust, $10-12.

Left: Orleans covered sugar in ivory, $15-20.

THE HOMER LAUGHLIN CHINA CO., NEWELL, W. VA.

PATTERN W-232

40

Carnival

Carnival was made for Quaker Oats as a promotional breakfast set. There were only five pieces; tea cup, saucer, fruit cup, six-inch plate, and oatmeal bowl. The shape was originally to have fluting, but that was changed to a pair of indented rings.

Carnival can be divided into two eras based on colors. The first, from the late 1930s and 1940s use the Fiesta glazes; cobalt, red, ivory, turquoise, green and yellow. The second, from the 1950s; gray, dark green, turquoise, and Harlequin yellow.

Carnival is almost never marked. It should be noted some pieces are easy to find in certain colors. For example, red fruit cups and saucers are not uncommon, but red teacups, six-inch plates and oatmeal bowls are next to impossible to locate. Cobalt and light green teacups are also hard to find.

Carnival cup, saucer and fruit bowl with original box. Cup and saucer, $6; box, $50+

The five Carnival shapes: 6" plate in dark green; teacup and saucer in turquoise; oatmeal bowl in Harlequin yellow; and fruit bowl in turquoise.

Far left: Two Carnival teacups in ivory and Fiesta yellow.; and **Near left**: One of several known Carnival teacups in a light yellow glaze that is similar to OvenServe's melon yellow.

Carnival 6" plates, $3-4.

Carnival Oatmeal bowls, $3-4.

Carnival cup in gray and saucer in Harlequin yellow, $5-6.

Original sketches of Carnival backstamps. These were never used, but some rare examples from the 1950s have a Carnival with star marking.

The rust colored saucer to the left is from Knowles' Deanna shape. It is shown with a Carnival saucer in light green since the two shapes are often confused with one another.

42

Colorama

Colorama was made in the 1960s for a short period of time. The flatware is a standard coupe shape, but the hollowware was specially designed. The finials should look familiar to HLC collectors as they were borrowed from Swing, a line that had been discontinued some twenty years prior.

Large pieces, such as plates and platters, are marked with the Colorama backstamp. Expect to find this line in single color sets rather than mixed colors.

Colorama 10" plate with sugar and creamer in pastel blue. Plate, $2-3, sugar, $3-5, and creamer, $2-3.

Coronet

The Coronet shape was available from 1935 until the 1940s. It is distinguished by its heavily embossed paneled rim and floral ring around the verge. There were several types of decorations applied to the Coronet shape; silver stamps, hand-painted treatments on the embossing, decals, under glaze patterns, and solid colors.

Coronet in solid colors are generally found in single color sets and in the Depression glazes; yellow (same Yellow used in Wells and Oven Serve), Sea Green, and ivory.

Coronet is often marked with a special back stamp with its shape name.

Coronet plates in Ming Green, $8-10.

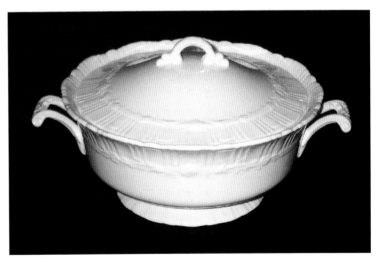

Coronet covered casserole in ivory, $45-50.

Dover

The Dover shape, sometimes called "White Dover" or "Colonial White", was offered from 1965 until the early 1980s. The paneled shape was used for decals, but single colored sets are not uncommon. Two glazes were used from the reissue Harlequin line; green and yellow. A rich brown was also used and marked, "Amberstone" though this line has nothing in common with the Amberstone that used Fiesta shapes.

Dover hollowware was never marked. Flatware may have a general HLC backstamp and date code.

Dover "Amberstone" 10" plate and 7" plate in green. Dinner plate, $3-4; 7" plate, $1-2.

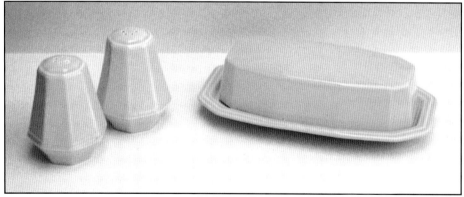

Dover covered butter and shakers in yellow. Butter, $6-7; shakers, $3-4 pr.

Dover sauceboat in Fiesta red. UND

Full assortment of Dover.

Epicure

Epicure was offered by Homer Laughlin in 1955. The heavy body oven proof ware was made in four colors; turquoise blue, charcoal gray, dawn pink, and snow white. The blue, gray, and pink glazes have a textured look similar to TST's Pebbleford which uses small iron filings in the glaze.

Epicure is almost always marked and can be differentiated by other 1950s shapes by its dropped edge. The shape was designed by HLC's art director at the time, Don Sheckengost. It was given a modern feel with no pedestal feet or applied finials.

In very rare cases, white Epicure can be found with decals.

Epicure 6" plates in charcoal, turquoise, and pink, $4-5.

Epicure coffeepot in turquoise, $200+

Epicure creamer and cereal bowls. Creamer, $10-12; cereal, $18-20.

Epicure individual casserole and covered casserole in pink. Individual casserole, $50-60; covered casserole, $70-80.

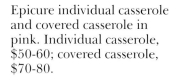

Epicure covered casserole in turquoise, $70-80.

Epicure tid-bit in white, $65-70.

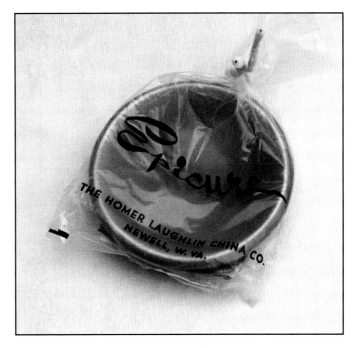

Epicure nut dish in original bag, $30-35

An Epicure Advertisement from 1955.

Assorted pieces from Kenilworth.

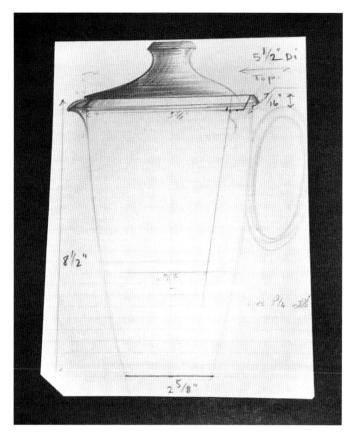

Original drawing for the Epicure coffeepot

Original drawing for Epicure lid and finial.

Fiesta

Fiesta was offered by Homer Laughlin from 1936 until 1973. It was reintroduced in 1986 and continues to be produced today. Based on pottery from Mexico and southern California, the round ring shape was designed by Frederick Rhead. The extensive color and item assortment changed over the years.

In the late 1960s, several lines were offered based on the Fiesta shapes. The supermarket promotions Sheffield Amberstone in brown and Coventry Casualstone in gold used Fiesta flatware with under glaze designs. The hollowware was restyled with a more contemporary feel.

In 1969, the restyled Fiesta from Amberstone and Casualstone was used for Fiesta Ironstone. This line was offered until 1973 and came in antique gold and turf green. Red was offered until 1972 and renamed, "mango red."

When Fiesta was reintroduced in 1986, many of the restyled pieces were used along with vintage shapes such as bulb candleholders and tripod candle holders (now called pyramids). As with the older Fiesta line, colors and items have come and gone over the past twenty years.

Fiesta 9" plates in yellow and light green.
The green plate sports the standard Fiesta backstamp used for most of the original production run, $15-20.

Fiesta 9" and 6" plates in light green, cobalt, yellow, and turquoise. 9" Plates, $15-20; 6", $8-10.

Fiesta demitasse coffeepot and regular coffeepot in yellow. Demitasse cup and saucer in red and teacup and saucer in cobalt.

Fiesta 11 ¾" fruit bowl in cobalt, $250-275.

Fiesta 5 ½" and 4 ¾" fruit bowls in red, $25-30.

Fiesta 2-pt. jug in gray, $130+

Fiesta 8" deep plate
in cobalt, $40-45.

Fiesta large teapot in red
and medium teapot in
turquoise. Large teapot,
$250-260; medium teapot,
$200-225.

Fiesta relish tray in the six
original colors with a metal
handle, $300-350.

Fiesta Amberstone coffeepot
(left) and regular coffeepot in
gray (right). Vintage coffeepot,
$300-325.

Fiesta carafe with lid in ivory. Far right is the contemporary version in sapphire. It lacks a pronounced foot and doesn't come with a lid. It also differs from the older version by the rings around its neck. Vintage carafe, $200-225.

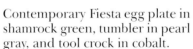

Fiesta covered casserole in ivory, $200-225.

Contemporary Fiesta egg plate in shamrock green, tumbler in pearl gray, and tool crock in cobalt.

Far left: These teacups are newer versions in periwinkle and cobalt. They were made from the Ironstone molds where the teacups have "C" handles. **Near left**: The older style has a full ring for handles. The older Fiesta teacups also have inside rings.

Contemporary Fiesta monarch vases in cobalt and sunflower yellow.

An assortment of new Fiesta pieces in sunflower yellow, plum, cinnabar, tangerine, and shamrock.

Contemporary Fiesta handled trays. The sea mist green in the back has the original style handles. The chartreuse example has the closed handle version.

Right: Contemporary Fiesta teacups in apricot and periwinkle, 10" vase in rose, tumbler in sapphire, disc pitcher in lilac, and shaker in chartreuse.

Contemporary Fiesta snack plate in persimmon, pyramid candleholder in turquoise, mini disc pitcher in rose, and mug in cobalt.

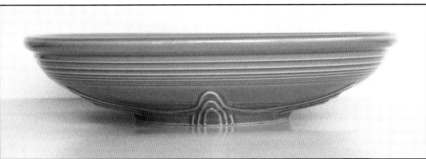

Contemporary Fiesta presentation bowl in turquoise.

Contemporary Fiesta platters in turquoise and persimmon.

Contemporary Fiesta bud vase in cobalt and 10" medium vase in lilac.

Contemporary Fiesta pedestal mug in turquoise, small bowl in rose, sauceboat in pearl gray.

Contemporary Fiesta bowls in turquoise and sunflower yellow.

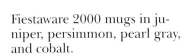

Fiestaware 2000 mugs in juniper, persimmon, pearl gray, and cobalt.

Fiesta bowls: towards the left in red and gray are vintage bowls; those to the right in chartreuse and turquoise are newer versions.

Contemporary Fiesta in scarlet: individual creamer, 8" vase, and cappuccino mug.

An assortment of Fiesta Amberstone.
From left to right; 6" plate, coffeepot, sauceboat stand, covered casserole, covered butter, ashtray, covered sugar, pie plate, fruit cup.

Detail of the Sheffield Amerberstone (left) and Covenetry Casualstone (left) patterns.

Experimental speckled glaze on a new Fiesta teacup and saucer.

Experimental Rose Ebony glaze on a vintage Fiesta carafe base. UND

Vintage Fiesta collection

Left: vintage Fiesta shaker in yellow. Right: Hall China kitchenware shaker in Chinese red.

Contemporary Fiesta medium vase in lilac.

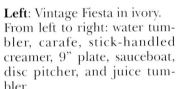

Left: Vintage Fiesta in ivory. From left to right: water tumbler, carafe, stick-handled creamer, 9" plate, sauceboat, disc pitcher, and juice tumbler.

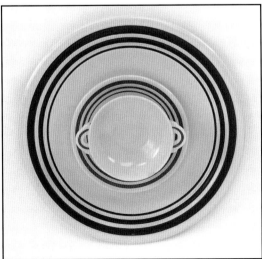

Left: Vintage Fiesta chop plate, 7" plate and cream soup cup in ivory with stripes. *Courtesy of Candy Fagerlin*.

Harlequin

Harlequin was made as an exclusive for F. W. Woolworth's in 1936. It was initially offered in four colors; maroon, yellow, green (spruce), and a medium blue, but, as with Fiesta, the colors and assortment changed over the years.

Though not marked, the shape is unmistakable. Most hollowware is conical with sharp angular handles. The flatware has a set of rings at the verge (where the rim meets the well). For a full assortment listing along with available colors, see the section on values.

Harlequin was discontinued in 1964. It was reissued in 1979 in four colors; turquoise, yellow, coral, and green. The new line had a very limited assortment. Many of the reissue plates and bowls can be found with HLC's backstamp.

Reissue Harlequin sugar in yellow and original sugar in red.

Novelty creamer in red and large cup in turquoise. The large cup was made in 1950s along with an oversized saucer measuring 6 7/8" in diameter. Novelty creamer, $20-25; large "jumbo" cup, $300+.

Harlequin sugar in red and regular creamer in turquoise. Sugar, $25-30; creamer, $7-9.

Harlequin double eggcups in yellow, red, medium blue, and rose, $12-20

Harlequin 36s bowl in rose, candleholder in spruce green, and high lip creamer in burgundy. The high lip creamer shown is the first style. The second style has a larger lip. It was replaced by what collectors call the regular creamer.

Harlequin individual or "toy" creamers. $20-25

Harlequin shakers with an all over gold decoration.

Harlequin ball jug. $35-45.

Right: Ring pattern on the bottom of the Harlequin ball jug.
Just about every pottery made some type of ball jug in different colored glazes. The ring pattern towards the base of the Harlequin ball jug is unique.

Right:
This drawing from HLC's archives show a proposed design for the inside of a Harlequin teacup. The bottom of the design says, "The Wishing Well Cup of Fortune."

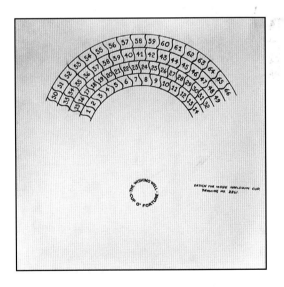

Harlequin teapot and covered casserole. Teapot, $110-$125; casserole, $75-85. *Courtesy of Fred Mutchler.*

Harlequin oval baker with teacup and saucer. Baker, $12-15; cup and saucer, $9-12.

In the background is a Harlequin 10" plate in turquoise. Its rings are in the "ball" of the plate — where the rim meets the well. It is shown with a vintage Fiesta carafe in ivory, demitasse cup in red, Lu-Ray creamer in Persian Cream, Pebbleford sugar in pink, and contemporary Fiesta tumbler in sapphire, and mug in juniper.

Jade

Jade was a formal square shape first made in 1931. There were two forms of Jade; Clair de Lune – a very pale green glaze, and Ivory – a plain vellum glaze first developed for the Century shape. In almost every case, Jade is found with decals, but it is included here as many undecorated examples can be found in both vellum and Clair de Lune glazes.

Jade teapot in a true red glaze. UND

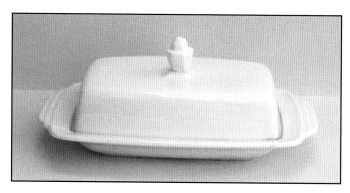

Jade shape butter in ivory. The Jade butter became a pickup piece for many of HLC's solid color and decal lines, $30-35.

Jubilee

In 1948, HLC produced the Jubilee shape. It was originally named Pageant, but was changed to Jubilee to celebrate HLC's seventy-fifth anniversary. It came in four solid colors; Celadon Green, Mist Gray, Cream Beige, and Shell Pink. Besides Jubilee, the pastel glazes were used on the Fiesta juice set and the Kitchen Kraft mixing bowls, but not on any other HLC shape.

In comparison to other pastel lines of the time, Jubilee was not a very good seller. There were three other lines that used the Jubilee shapes; Debutante – white with decals, Skytone – blue clay with contrasting white finals and handles, and Suntone – similar to Skytone, but with brown clay. Of the four, Skytone is the easiest to find today and was made with and without decals.

Each of the four lines are marked with appropriate backstamps.

Jubilee 6" plate in pink and creamer in beige. Plate, $5-6; creamer, $6-8.

Jubilee coffeepot in gray, $30-35.

Jubilee covered sugar in gray and cup and saucer in green. Sugar $8-10, cup and saucer $8-10.

Jubilee demitasse cup and saucer in pink and fruit cup in beige. Demitasse cup and saucer, $19-23, $5-6.

The gravy fast stand on the left is the standard version. It was made by attaching the bowl to the base then glazing. The one on the right is not a standard item as it lacks the base. Standard gravy, $10-12.

Fiesta juice set in the four Jubilee colors.

Original drawing for Jubilee with the name Pageant.

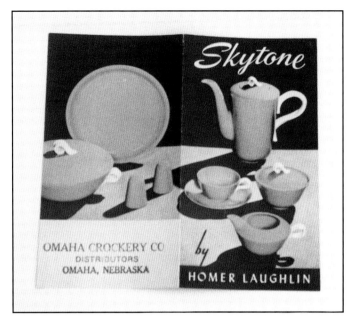

Skytone brochure.

Skytone 10" plate with decal, $8-10

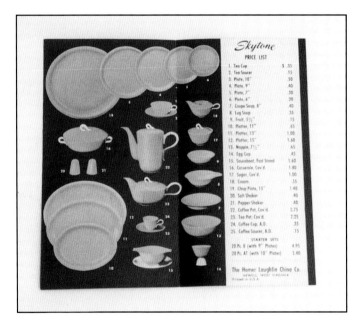

Skytone brochure.

Suntone double eggcup, $12-15.

Kraft Blue

The Kraft Blue line is made up of 'rope' embossed shapes in a powder blue clay. The handles and finials were done in contrasting white and the whole piece was then given a clear glaze. This process was later repeated on the Jubilee shape to create Skytone.

Kraft Blue was created in 1937 as a Woolworth's exclusive. On September 15, 1937, Frederick Rhead noted in his journal possible names for the then new line; Blue Rope, Cadet, Blue Body, Lyric, Chalet, Blue Danube, and Iris. It wasn't until the thirtieth of the same month that the Kraft Blue name was decided upon.

Kraft Blue continued to be produced until the early 1950s and sometimes is decorated in the decals available during the same time as Skytone.

A pink clay version exists, aptly named Kraft Pink.

Kraft Blue teapot, $20-35.

Kraft Pink covered sugar, $8-12.

Kraft Blue creamer and Kraft Pink bowl. Creamer, $4-9; bowl, $6-8.

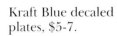

Kraft Blue decaled plates, $5-7.

Left: Harlequin novelty creamer. Right: Kraft Blue and Kraft Pink novelty creamers. Harlequin creamer, $30-35; Kraft Blue and Pink creamers, $25-40.

Fruit Skin Glazes cup and saucer and dinner plate. UND

Fruit Skin Glazes covered onion soup with liner; and cup and saucer. UND

Fruit Skin Glazes onion soup base. UND

65

Peasant Ware 10" plate; 7" plate and cup and saucer.

OVAL FAST STAND BOAT WITH ROPE HANDLE

Original sketch for proposed rope shape fast stand.

Peasant Ware teapot, $50+

Nautilus

The decal shape, Nautilus, was made from 1935 until the early 1950s. In early 1940, the Nautilus shapes were dipped in the Serenade pastel glazes and sold through Woolworth's. Two changes to the regular Nautilus line were made for Pastel Nautilus. A larger teacup was created and an egg cup was added. The egg cup was from the Kraft Blue shape minus the rope embossing.

Pastel Nautilus can be found with a general HLC backstamp and date code.

Nautilus covered casserole in pink, $20-25.

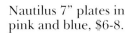

Nautilus 7" plates in pink and blue, $6-8.

Nautilus sauceboat in pink, $6-8.

Eggcups in pink and blue. These were not part of the standard Nautilus line. They were made especially for the pastel Nautilus version by taking the Kraft Blue eggcups and removing the rope embossing. $6-8.

Left: Nautilus teacup; right, Fiesta teacup. Both are in the brown glaze from Sheffield Amberstone.

Nautilus 10" plate glazed in turquoise and decorated with cobalt design. This piece was made at the Newell Art Classes – a pottery class offered by HLC in the late 1930s. UND

Newell Art Class Nautilus plate marking. UND

Old Roman

Old Roman started out as a promotional breakfast set for Quaker Oats and expanded into a full dinnerware service in the early 1930s. It was made either in a light yellow glaze or green. The yellow pieces are usually found with decals or with the embossed trim highlighted in green. The solid green pieces never have decals.

There were several markings used on Old Roman. Most are marked simply, "Old Roman" with no other information as to maker or date code. Some are marked Old Roman with a patent number. Finally, some pieces are marked with the Wells Art Glazes backstamp.

Old Roman 9" plate and creamer. Plate, $12-15; creamer, $15-18.

Old Roman 9" plate in yellow with green wash border, $12-15.

Old Roman square plate in green, $18-20.

Old Roman 9" plate and cup and saucer. Plate, $12-15; cup and saucer, $17-25.

Old Roman Square
plate in yellow with
decal, $18-20.

Old Roman creamer and sugar.
Front: Newell shape A.D. sugar.
Creamer, $15-18; sugar, $20-25,
and Newell AD sugar, $18-20.

Old Roman saucer with WAG marking.

Trellis shape 6" plate in green, $6-7.

Newell shape casserole in yellow with decals, $30-35.

Old Roman cup and saucer, $17-25.

OvenServe

OvenServe was a combination kitchenware-dinnerware line made by Homer Laughlin from 1933 until the mid-1940s. The embossed shape was decorated with decals, hand-painted treatments and decals. The most common OvenServe treatment is the green hand-painted embossing sold through Woolworth's. There were two solid colors used for OvenServe; melon yellow (the same yellow used in Wells Art Glazes) and orange, a.k.a. "pumpkin."

In the 1950s, Quaker Oats offered five small Oven-Serve pieces as promotions in their boxes of oats. The assortment included; custard, ramekin, cereal bowl, oval baker, and the small French casserole. Quaker Oats never wanted to rely solely on one supplier so Taylor Smith & Taylor shared in producing the five smaller items. The only difference in shapes between the two involves the handled casserole. HLC's was made as a bowl with an applied handle. TST's was modeled as one piece.

Quaker Oats OvenServe can be found in turquoise, dark green, yellow, pink, brown. Some TST colors that HLC never used often show up such as a sage green, and the speckled glazes Turquoise and Marble (white). The Quaker Oats OvenServe will bear with the appropriate maker's markings.

OvenServe casserole in pumpkin with black trim, $15-18.

OvenServe batter
jug, $75-95.

OvenServe shirred egg dish
and bowl. Shirred egg dish,
$18-20; bowl, $8-12.

OvenServe fish platter
in yellow, $12-15.

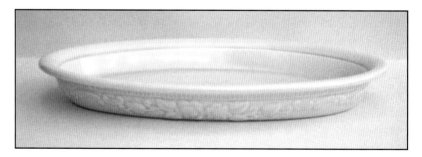

OvenServe small
baker in pink, $4-5.

OvenServe shirred egg dish in pumpkin, ramekin in brown, custard in yellow.

OvenServe leftover without embossing in turquoise and with embossing in ivory with hand-painted accents.

Bottoms of OvenServe leftovers.

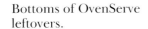

OvenServe cake server in yellow, fork in turquoise, long spoon in turquoise, short spoon in yellow.

OvenServe short spoon
in pumpkin, $50-60.

OvenServe 40-oz.
teapot in pumpkin,
$300+

OvenServe 16-oz. Teapot
in an odd green glaze,
$300+

Mother's Oats box
featuring OvenServe,
$35-40.

Chromatic OvenServe pitcher
in pink. UND.

Chromatic OvenServe mark-
ing. UND.

Riviera

Riviera dinnerware was created in 1938 using pieces from the already existing Century line. The square shape was originally made in 1931 as an extensive line so there are more pieces in Century than Riviera. Four colors were initially used; Harlequin yellow, blue, light green, and red. When red was discontinued in 1943, ivory took its place.

While most of the assortment came from Century, some pieces were specially created for Riviera such as the quarter-pound butter, juice pitcher, and juice tumblers. Two pieces created but never officially produced were the console bowl and candlesticks.

The shakers were picked up from Tango and the half-pound butter came from Jade.

Riviera was sold through G.C. Murphy's, Newberry's, Sears, and a host of other retailers. By the early 1950s, it was discontinued.

Sometimes Riviera can be found with a foil sticker and, in some instances, with a USA marking.

Assortment of Riviera dishes.

Riviera flatware.

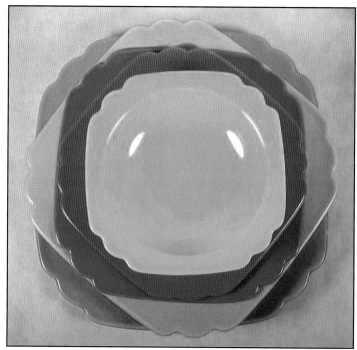

Riviera deep plates in medium blue, red, green, and yellow, $8-10.

Riviera cup and saucer in red, $13-16.

Riviera 7" plate in cobalt, $18-20.

Riviera sugar in green with HLC backstamp. Very few pieces of Riviera were marked. It's believed they were given the HLC USA marking when exported to Canada.

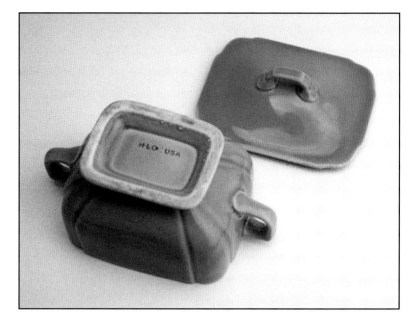

Riviera ¼-lb butter dish in red, $125-150.

Century shape cream soup cup in ivory. These were not part of the standard Riviera line, but one in yellow and one in cobalt have been found.

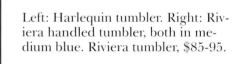

Left: Harlequin tumbler. Right: Riviera handled tumbler, both in medium blue. Riviera tumbler, $85-95.

Original Riviera price list.

SQUARE
"BOHEMIA" WARE

24-PC. SET—4 COLORS

With this set, the table can be
set with each place a different
color . . . or the colors can be
scrambled, cup one color, saucer
another color. Color is exciting,
and how it sells!

Made by Homer Laughlin. Colors similar
to those of the popular "Fiesta" ware.
Set consists of: 4 cups, four 6 in. saucers,
four 6⅛ in. plates, four 9 in. plates, four
5¼ in. fruit saucers—each in red, blue,
yellow and green, 1 yellow vegetable dish,
1 green open sugar, 1 red creamer and one
12x9 in. blue dish.

55R-6000—1 set in pkg.
18 lbs. . . . . Set **3.75**

Riviera dishes sold as "Bohemia" ware
in a 1940s wholesale catalog.

Century Batter jug, syrup jug, A.D. sugar, and A.D creamer in ivory with the
Black Tulip decal.

NO. 1

NO. 2

Original drawings for
Riviera foil stickers.

NO. 3

NO. 4

Drawing No. 2424
Mar. 2, 1940

Rhythm

Rhythm was made during the 1950s. HLC followed suit of other potteries making plain round coupe shapes and introduced both Jubilee and Rhythm as a result. While Jubilee was given pastel colors, Rhythm was done in bold colors common in the 50s; burgundy, yellow, gray, dark green, and chartreuse. The shape was also used with decals and other types of decoration such as under glaze Dura-Prints.

Most pieces are marked with a Rhythm backstamp and date code.

Rhythm plates in dark green and gray, $6-8.

Left: Rhythm original creamer in burgundy and water jug in white. Creamer, $6-8; jug, $18-20.

Below:
Rhythm sauceboats in turquoise and brown. These were used with the Charm House line. They are shown along with a Charm House creamer in yellow. Sauceboats, $5-7; Charm House creamer, $4-5.

Swing shape shakers were picked up and used with Rhythm. Here they are glazed in yellow, $6-8.

Rhythm restyled creamer and covered sugar in gray. Tall creamer, $4-6; sugar, $6-8.

Charm House cup, saucer and covered sugar in cobalt. Cup and saucer, $6-7; sugar $6-8.

Charm House covered casserole in dark green, $30-35.

Large Salad bowl. These are not officially part of the Rhythm line, but they are often found in salad sets consisting of the large bowl in dark green and small Rhythm bowls in chartreuse, $50-60.

Rhythm divided snack plate in dark green, $30-35.

Serenade Kitchen
Kraft marking.

ROYAL'S "PYREX-SERENADE"

Glowing Color *Plus* Visibility

An entirely new idea in casseroles that is both beautiful and practical; a smart pastel-colored "Serenade"
pottery bowl with a transparent PYREX top! Women
love color because it enlivens the table . . . and they
are sure to admire the clear glass top because a mere
glance tells how the food is baking. The pottery bowls
come in four pastel shades: pink, blue, yellow and
white. Stunning chrome frame of tasteful design for
table service. Completely ovenproof combination with
plenty of sales appeal.

"PYREX" is a registered trade-mark of Corning Glass Works, Corning, N. Y.
"SERENADE" is a registered trade-mark of Homer-Laughlin China Co., Newell, W. Va.

No. 39-13 CASSEROLE

Packed one color to the one dozen unit
. . . your choice of white, yellow, pink
or blue. Shipped complete from one
plant; weight about 50 lbs. per dozen.

ROYAL METAL MANUFACTURING COMPANY, 1138 S. MICHIGAN BLVD., CHICAGO, ILLINOIS

Tango

Tango is a combination petal and scallop shape first created in 1936. It was originally released in the Harlequin colors; blue, green, maroon, and yellow. When maroon was discontinued in the early 1940s, it was replaced by Fiesta red.

The assortment to Tango is limited to seventeen items. No teapot or sauceboat were created for Tango, though records indicate a cream soup cup was modeled, but not released into production.

Tango was never marked.

Tango plates in yellow and spruce green. 10", $18-20; 7", $10-12.

Tango deep plate in burgundy; and the covered sugar and creamer in spruce. Deep plate, $12-15, sugar, $18-20, and creamer, $12-15.

Tango platter in burgundy and baker, spruce. Platter and baker, both $18-20.

Tango creamer and sugar in burgundy. Sugar, $18-20; creamer, $12-15. *Courtesy of Eva Zia.*

Tango teacup and saucer in medium blue and Republic shape demitasse cup and saucer in red. Teacup and saucer $16-20; demitasse cup and saucer, $55-65.

Left: original style Tango teacup, right: Tango teacup with restyled handle.

Tango shakers in blue and red. This shape was also used in the Riviera line, $8-10. *Courtesy of Fred Mutchler.*

86

Theme

Theme was made by Homer Laughlin from 1939 until the 1950s. The molded relief was inspired by Jasperware by Wedgwood & Sons of England. In fact, the original design called for the embossing to be done in blue clay then added to plain Nautilus shapes in white complete with a clear glaze. After some trials, it was decided the embossing would be part of the Theme molds and not added as it is done with Jasperware.

Theme was meant for decals and under glaze transfers, but once in a while solid colors can be found, namely Harlequin's spruce green and Fiesta's turquoise and cobalt. Hopefully, more solid color glazes will be found as they bring the embossing on the rim to life. Theme blanks (white with no decals) are not uncommon.

Pieces are almost always marked with a special Theme backstamp.

Theme Eggshell 9" plates in turquoise and spruce, 35-40.

Theme Eggshell gravy fast stand in white, $15-18.

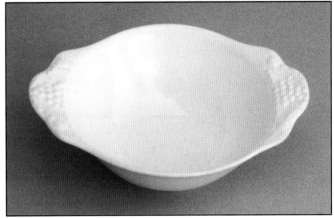

Theme Eggshell lug soup in white, $8-10.

Theme Eggshell square plates in pearlized glazes. These were most likely decorated by an outside company, $10-12.

Virginia Rose

Virginia Rose was one of Homer Laughlin's longest running shapes having been made from late 1932 until circa 1968. In almost every case, it is found with decals, but a few pieces have turned up in solid colored glazes so it is included in this book.

Virginia Rose blanks are not uncommon, but the gold glazes from the late 1960s are rare. So far, only a handful of pieces have been found in at least three different gold glazes. Most Virginia Rose has a backstamp, but the gold glazed versions are unmarked.

Virginia Rose covered sugar in gold glaze from the late 1960s, $50-60.

Virginia Rose coffeepot, and covered sugar and creamer in gold. Coffeepot, $125, sugar, $50-60, creamer, $45-50.

Wells

Wells was made in the early 1930s — a time when dinnerware was made in single color sets rather than "rainbow" or mixed colors. The glazes included; French Rose, Leaf Green, Mellon Yellow, and Sienna Brown. Some pieces can be found in a Fiesta red type glaze as well as a blue. Ivory Wells turns up from time to time, but these are thought to be undecorated blanks.

The Wells shape itself was used not only for solid colors, but also decals and banded treatments. The solid colors generally have a Wells Art Glazes backstamp whereas the decaled pieces have the Wells peacock decal mark.

Wells dinner plate and covered sugar in rust.

Wells teapot in a glaze very similar to Fiesta red. Other pieces have been found in this glaze, namely demitasse cups, saucers, and a creamer.

Wells fruit cups in rose and an Empress shape teapot in blue. The Empress shape teapot can be found in the blue glaze as well as yellow. They often have the Wells Art Glazes marking. Fruit cups, $4-5; Empress teapot, $125+.

Nautilus shape lug soup in WAG rose, $8-10.

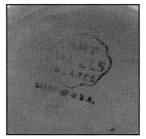

Markings on the Wells Art Glazes batter jug and decaled syrup.

Wells batter jug in rose and a decaled Wells syrup pitcher. Batter jug, $65-75; syrup, $55-65.

Original drawings for proposed Wells backstamps.

Chapter Nine

Mount Clemens Pottery Company

Mt. Clemens, Michigan (1915 - 1987)

Production began at Mount Clemens Pottery Company (MCPCo) in January of 1915 under the management of Charles E. Doll. The S.S. Kresge Company bought the company in 1920. They eventually sold in 1965, and the pottery was renamed the Jamestown China Company. In 1983, Action Industries of Cheswick, Pennsylvania assumed control. In 1987, the pottery was finally closed.

The most popular of MCPCo's lines was Petal. It was made in solid colors with green being the most popular. Many of Mt. Clemens' shapes can be found with Stetson China's backstamp since they would often buy Mt. Clemens' blanks.

Oxford shape sauceboat in yellow, scalloped shape 36s bowls in blue. Sauceboat, $8-10; 36s bowl, $10-12.

Panneled shape 36s bowls in burgundy and green. The raised USA marking on the center bowl is typical of some of Mt. Clemens' wares, $10-12.

A.D. sugar and creamer in blue, $4-6.

A.D. sugar and cream-
er in burgundy, $4-6.

Alara

Alara, from the Latin "alaris" meaning "wings", was made by Mt. Clemens and was sold to the Stetson Pottery Company who would decorate blanks with decal treatments. The shape was also used in the same solid colors MCPCo used for Petal; maroon, green, blue, and yellow. However, solid color Alara is much more difficult to find than Petal.

Yellow pieces can be found blank or with decals. It is very rare for Alara, solid color or otherwise, to be found marked.

Alara platter in yellow, $10-12.

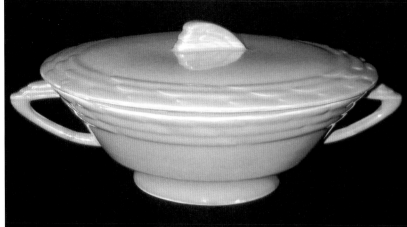

Alara covered casserole in blue, $20-25.

Alara creamer in burgundy, $6-8.

Mt. Clemens backstamp with the intertwined litters: MCPCo. This is usually found on larger Petal items such as platters and dinner plates.

Petal

Petal was made by Mt. Clemens in the 1930s and 1940s. The shape is called Toulon and can be found in solid colors, plain white, and with decal treatments. Maroon and green are the easiest colors to find. Yellow is difficult to find and may be simply undecorated blanks. The blue is a deep rich sapphire color with a matte finish.

The flatware may be marked with the Mt. Clemens backstamp and date code. Hollowware often has a raised USA mold mark.

Besides green, maroon, yellow, and blue, Petal has been found in turquoise, pink and brown.

Petal 9" plate, fruit cup, and teacup in burgundy. The 7" plate in blue.

Petal 9" plate in green, 6" plate in burgundy, and teacup in blue.

Petal platters in green, sauce-boat in yellow. Platters, $10-12; sauceboat, $8-10.

Petal covered butter in green, $20-25.

Petal covered casserole in green, $20-25.

Petal creamer and sugar in green. Creamer, $6-8; sugar, $8-10.

Petal serving bowl in turquoise, $7-9.

Petal serving bowl in pink, $7-9.

Vogue

Vogue is a heavily embossed line from the 1930s and 1940s. It can be found in white, both with and without decals, but sometimes solid color pieces turn up. The milk jug in green is quite common and is marked with an embossed U.S.A.

Stetson purchased Vogue blanks from Mt. Clemens and decorated them. The Stetson name for this shape is "Annette."

Vogue milk pitcher in green, $12-15.

Chapter Ten

Paden City Pottery Company
Paden City, West Virginia (1914 - 1963)

Paden City produced dinnerware and kitchenware. One of its more collectible wares is the Mexican-theme decal, Patio which was used on their Shell Krest and Bak-Serve, a kitchenware line. They also made a pastel colored line using the plain round Shenandoah shape. These colors include pink, blue, green, and yellow.

Caliente

Caliente used bold Fiesta-type glazes. Montgomery Wards listed these colors in 1940 as; tangerine, yellow, blue, and green. The blue is a deep cobalt and the green is more of a turquoise shade. Caliente can also be found in pastel glazes.

Caliente used shapes from several of Paden City's lines. Most pieces come from Shell Krest — namely those with sea shell finials and tab handles. Plain round shapes come from the "New Virginia" shape. And a host of different shapes of casseroles and bowls made up the Caliente kitchenware.

Caliente Advertisement

Caliente assorted flatware
and shakers.

Caliente chop plate in red, 9"
plate in turquoise, and coupe
soup in cobalt.

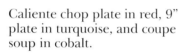

Caliente Mixing bowls,
$15-20 ea.

Caliente teapot in
cobalt, $30-35.

Caliente candleholders in cobalt, $25-35 pr.

Calienete candleholders in red, $25-35 pr.

Caliente casserole in cobalt, $20-25.

New Virginia shape creamer and sugar in cobalt. Sugar, $8-10; creamer, $6-8.

Chapter Eleven

Red Wing
Red Wing, Minnesota (1906-1967)

In the late 1930s, Red Wing created four sets of dinnerware lines and marketed them as Gypsy Trail Hostess Ware. Designed by Belle Kogan, they are; Plain, Chevron, Fondoso, and Reed. Here we look at examples of two of the more common lines, Fondoso and Reed.

Fondoso teacup and saucer, $11-14.

Fondoso salt and pepper shakers, $18-20 pr. *Courtesy of Eva Zia.*

Fondoso covered casserole in cobalt, $35-40. *Courtesy of Eva Zia.*

Fondoso teacup and
saucer in red, $11-14.

Fondoso covered casserole,
$35-40. *Courtesy of Terri Puleo.*

Reed covered casserole in turquoise. $20-25. *Courtesy of Eva Zia.*

Reed double eggcup in red,
$10-12. *Courtesy of Eva Zia.*

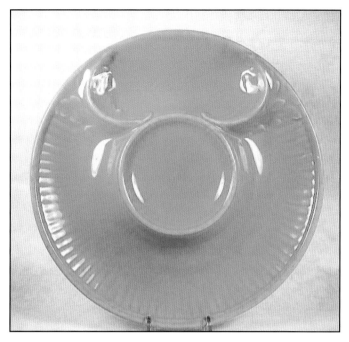

Reed turquoise -compartment dish, $25-30.
Courtesy of Eva Zia.

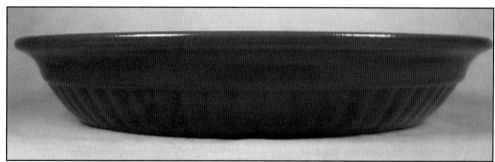

Reed pie plate in cobalt, $15-18. *Courtesy of Eva Zia.*

Reed gravy fast stand, $20-25. *Courtesy of Eva Zia.*

Reed novelty creamer in red, $18-20. *Courtesy of Eva Zia.*

Reed teapot, sugar, and creamer in red. Teapot, $45-50, sugar, $6-8, and creamer, $4-5. *Courtesy of Terri Puleo.*

Reed teapot in cobalt, $45-50. *Courtesy of Terri Puleo.*

Reed covered syrup in green, $20-30. *Courtesy of Terri Puleo.*

Reed covered syrup in turquoise, $20-30. *Courtesy of Terri Puleo.*

Chapter Twelve
Royal China Company
Sebring, Ohio (1933 - 1986)

Royal China is most famous for its many under glaze treatments, but they started out making common semi-vitreous dinnerware like every other pottery in the 1930s and 40s. Some of their more popular shapes are Swirl, Oxford, Windsor, Royalty, Regent, and Regal. Later shapes included Futura and Royal Stone.

Swirl & Blue Gaiety

Royal China's Blue Gaiety was offered through Montgomery Wards in the late 1940s as, "…one of the most unusual patterns we have seen, charming and unique because no two pieces are exactly alike. A vibrant blue provides a bright background for tracing of old gold color, the antique effect different on every piece. The swirl design on the rim of the plate is repeated on each piece in the set."

Royal China covered sugar in pastel pink. These, along with other hollowware, were also made in turquoise and mixed into decal lines of the late 1950s, $5-6.

Blue Gaiety teapot, $20-25.

Blue Gaiety covered sugar, $7-9.

Swirl teapot in blue, $20-25. *Courtesy of Terri Puleo*.

Swirl covered sugar in yellow and creamer in blue. Sugar, $7-9; creamer, $3-4.
Courtesy of Terri Puleo.

Chapter Thirteen

Sebring Pottery Co., American Limoges China Company, and Leigh Potters, Inc.

Sebring Pottery, American Limoges, and Leigh Potters were all owned by The Sebring family. Because of this, many shapes were shared and the backstamps can vary from piece to piece. For example, the Snowflake shape originated with American Limoges, but often decaled pieces will carry the Leigh Ware backstamp.

Aristocrat

Aristocrat was a short-lived line from the 1930s. When found, it is usually in solid colors or with colored bands. The bulbous shape of the hollowware made it a poor candidate for decals, but some decaled examples can be found today.

Aristocrat has been found in maroon, ivory, rust, cobalt and tangerine.

Aristocrat teapot in white, $40-50.

Aristocrat covered sugar in white with red trim, $12-15.
Courtesy of Terri Puleo.

Aristocrat open sugar
in cobalt, $12-15.

Aristocrat sauceboat with
gold stars and trim, $12-15.

Corinthian

The Corinthian shape was a formal-style line of dinnerware that used decal treatments. In the late 1930s, Corinthian was dipped in solid colors and sold as, "Rainbo Ware." (See advertisement on the right.)

Rainbo WARE   SEBRING

YOU DON'T HAVE TO TRAVEL
TO THE END OF THE RAIN-
BOW TO REALIZE PROFITS IN
RAINBO WARE.

Already in metropolitan stores
RAINBO WARE is making sales
soar. It is the sensation of the
pottery world.

New gorgeous colors—in the un-
derglaze colors that can never
wear off. Perfectly adaptable to
any size dinner set or occasion
and the price within the reach of
all. There is money in RAINBO
WARE.

— VARIETY — STYLE — PRICE —

Designs created by internationally famous
artists—Gale Turnbull, Olga Muench, and
many others including Jean Luce, the de-
signer of the dinnerware for the famous
Normandie.

● ● ●

A complete new showing of these wares
will be made at—
SPACE 619-620-621
HOTEL PENNSYLVANIA
NEW YORK HOUSEFURNISHING SHOW
July 19 - 25

SPACE 522
AMERICAN FURNITURE MART
CHICAGO FURNITURE SHOW
July 6 - 18

SPACE 615
AMERICAN FURNITURE EXCHANGE BLDG.
NEW YORK FURNITURE SHOW
July 20 - 31

MANUFACTURERS AND IMPORTERS
ASSOCIATES SHOW
BILTMORE HOTEL - First Floor
LOS ANGELES, CALIF.
ROOM 1350
August 2 - 7

MANUFACTURERS AND IMPORTERS
ASSOCIATES SHOW
ST. FRANCIS HOTEL - First Floor
LOS ANGELES, CALIF.
ROOM 216-211
August 10 - 16

TALENT TO CREATE — AND —
ABILITY TO PRODUCE

THE SEBRING POTTERY COMPANY
SEBRING   CHARLES L. SEBRING, President   OHIO

CROCKERY AND GLASS JOURNAL for July, 1936   15

Snowflake

Snowflake is very hard to find. To date, it has been found in medium blue, but other colors may exist. According to trade listings, this shape was offered in 1937 only. Its embossed pattern may have been too seasonal to be a favorite year round.

Snowflake covered sugar and creamer. Sugar, $12-15; creamer, $6-8.

Snowflake handled tray with Rose of Sharon decal, green wash trim, and gold filigree. This particular piece bears the Leigh Ware back-stamp, $8-10.

Snowflake handled tray with Rose of Sharon decal, yellow wash trim, and gold filigree, $8-10.

MASS PRODUCTION

The new Snowflake ware. An embossed shape inspired by snowflake motifs.

Triumph

Triumph was made from the late 1930s until the early 1950s. It was designed by Victor Sheckengost with horizontal fluting at the bottoms of hollowware and rings along the rims of flatware. Most of the time, Triumph is found with decals, but several solid colors have been found including, green, blue, dark green, yellow, ivory, and pink. Sometimes it is marked, "Cameo."

Triumph sauceboat in green, $8-10.

Triumph coffee server in dark green, $15-20. *Courtesy of Eva Zia.*

Chapter Fourteen

Sevilla Pottery

Sevilla was a line of kitchenware and novelty ware produced in the late 1930s until the very early 1950s. According to Lois Lehner, the Sevilla marking was filed by Cronin for registration on February 1938, claiming use since 1937.

Sevilla has been found in the following glazes; cobalt, medium blue, turquoise, red (over ivory), yellow, green, maroon, gray, pink, brown, and plain ivory. Larger pieces may be marked Sevilla in the mold, or have Cronin's "Bake Oven" raised marking. Smaller pieces generally have a completely dry foot with no marks.

It should be noted that a small ewer was recently found in blue with a "Souvenir of Cameron, WV" sticker. It may be possible that some of the Sevilla pieces, notably the smaller novelties, were made in Cameron since there are several trade listings with Cameron Clay Products as using the Sevilla name.

Perhaps the connection between Sevilla, Cronin, and Cameron can be cleared up in the future.

Sevilla teapot in medium blue, $15-20.

Sevilla teapot, $15-20.

Sevilla elephants in yellow and ivory, $8-10 ea.

Sevilla small flower pot, $6-8.

Sevilla shakers and creamer, $4-5.

Sevilla miniature ewers, $6-8.

Sevilla range set in gray,
$15-20.

Sevilla leafy style creamer
and sugar, $4-5.

Sevilla range set in
red, $15-20.

Sevilla mixing bowl
in pastel blue, $8-10.

111

Sevilla swan planters in cobalt and red, $8-10 ea.

Sevilla cookie jar in red, $15-20.

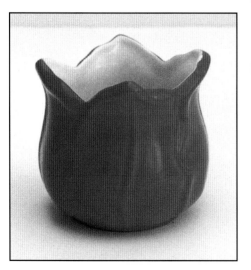

Sevilla juice set. The pitcher has a completely dry underside, unlike Fiesta's, which will be glazed and marked. Pitcher, $10-12; tumblers, $6-8.

Sevilla leafy planter, $8-10.

Sevilla teapot in red,
$15-20

Sevilla demitasse coffeepot in red, $15-20.

Sevilla miniature ewers, $6-8 ea.

Sevilla carafe, sugar, creamer
and ewer in red. Carafe, $10-12,
sugar and creamer, $4-5 ea., and
ewer, $10-12.

Sevilla heart shape vases in red and green, $8-10 ea.

Sevilla mixing bowls in burgundy, brown, and medium blue, $8-10 ea.

Sevilla disc pitchers in burgundy and green, $10-12 ea.

Sevilla ball sugar in cobalt and ball creamer in red, $4-5 ea.

Sevilla dog planter and lamb planter in blue. Shown is the smaller of two sizes of lamb planters, $8-10 ea.

Sevilla small vases in red, $6-8.

Sevilla duck planters, $8-10 ea.

Sevilla covered sugar and creamer, $4-5 ea. There is also a matching teapot.

Sevilla donkey planter, $8-10.

Chapter Fifteen

Shawnee Pottery Company
Zanesville, Ohio (1937 - 1961)

Shawnee made cookie jars, teapots, vases, planters, and other novelty ware. However, in the late 1930s, they made the solid colored line, Valencia.

Valencia

Valencia was offered by Shawnee and sold exclusively for Sears & Roebuck. Designed by Louse Bauer, the shape is characterized with a deep swirl along the rim of flatware and body of hollowware. It has an extensive assortment, but not all the pieces from old trade ads have been accounted for.

It can be found in green, cobalt, yellow, tangerine, maroon, ivory. Some pieces may be marked with U.S.A.

Floret covered teapot in blue, $20-25. These are often mistaken as Vistosa teapots because of the floral handle and finial.

Valencia ball jug in cobalt, plates in green and tangerine, tumblers in burgundy, pink, pastel blue, and shaker in yellow. *Courtesy of Terri Puleo.*

Late 1938 ad for Sears' Valencia.

Valencia carafe in tangerine, $85-95. *Courtesy of Eva Zia.*

Valencia batter jugs in tangerine and cobalt, $60-70. *Courtesy of Eva Zia.*

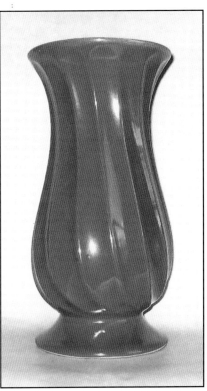

Valencia flower vase in tangerine, $90-100. *Courtesy of Eva Zia.*

117

Valencia sugar and creamer in tangerine. Sugar, $18-20; creamer, $8-10. *Courtesy of Eva Zia*.

Valencia cup and saucer in tangerine, $10-13. *Courtesy of Eva Zia*.

Valencia teapot in tangerine, $45-50. *Courtesy of Eva Zia*.

Valencia bowls in tangerine, yellow, and green. *Courtesy of Eva Zia*.

Valencia dinner plates
in tangerine and yellow,
$20-25.

Valencia shakers in yellow with original sticker, $15-20 pr.
From the collection of Dominick Abel, photo courtesy of Kathleen Moloney.

Valencia batter set.
From the collection of Dominick Abel, photo by Kathleen Moloney.

Valencia relish trays,
$145-165.
From the collection of Dominick Abel, photo by Kathleen Moloney.

119

Adam Antique

Adam Antique was one of Steubenville's longest running lines. It was first offered in the 1930s and lasted until the pottery closed in 1959. The heavily embossed shape was created for decals and other treatments, but plain ivory or white pieces are not uncommon.

Canonsburg Pottery of Canonsburg, Pennsylvania purchased the molds after Steubenville Pottery closed. They created an Ironstone line using Adam Antique shapes and called it, "Regency." It was offered in the 1960s and possibly in the early 1970s. At least two colors have been found: gold and olive green.

Adam Antique coffee pot, $40-45.

Adam Antique shakers, $8-10 pr.

Chapter Seventeen

Taylor, Smith & Taylor Company
Chester, West Virginia (1899 - 1981)

Taylor, Smith & Taylor, or TST, started out as Taylor, Smith & Lee in Chester, West Virginia in 1899. By 1901, Lee left the pottery and it became Taylor, Smith & Taylor. TST made hotel ware, toilet ware, kitchenware, and porcelain in its early years. By the late 1920s, most of their production focused on semi-porcelain dinnerware. They were one of the first potteries to produce wares in a colored body. In their case, it was a pink body they often marketed as, "Rose Mist." The pink body was used on several shapes including Paramount, Regal, Capitol, Garland, and Plymouth.

The most famous TST product was Lu-Ray Pastels which was made for almost twenty-five years. Collectors today also have gained appreciation for their 1950s Pebbleford line and various under glaze treatments.

Taylor, Smith & Taylor was bought out by Anchor Hocking in the early 1970s. The factory finally closed in 1981 and stands today in ruins.

Taylor, Smith & Taylor shapes and colors: Lu-Ray Pastels in surf green, Pebbleford in turquoise, Vogue in Sharon pink, Empire in Persian cream, and Conversation in chatham gray.

French Casseroles glazed in pastel blue and yellow with decals, $8-10.

Inside of the TST plant in the summer of 2000.

Remains of a TST kiln as seen in 2000.

Conversation

Designed by Walter Dorwin Teague, Conversation was made from 1948 until the mid 1950s. It was used primarily for decals. Four Lu-Ray colors were chosen to make up a special set for Montgomery Wards. The color assortment was Windsor Blue, Persian Cream, Sharon Pink, and Chatham Gray. In 1953, when Chatham Gray was no longer used, Surf Green served as a replacement until the Conversation line was discontinued all together. As a result, Surf Green Conversation is a little more difficult to find than the other four colors. (It should be noted this is not the case with Lu-Ray Pastels where gray is more difficult to find.)

The Conversation shape was one of the first to be offered in two-tone effects. The outsides of hollowware were often glazed in green, brown, or gray and combined with decaled flatware. There were also instances where colored glazed flatware, namely brown, was mixed with hand-painted pieces for effect.

Conversation can be found in Pebbleford glazes. Since Conversation was being phased out as Pebbleford was being developed, such pieces are rare.

Most Conversation is found marked with the shape name.

Conversation bowls in yellow, pink, and green.

Conversation sugar in blue and creamer in pink. Sugar, $8-10; creamer, $5-7.

Conversation sauceboat in yellow and stand in blue, $15-20.

Conversation platters in green and gray, $8-10.

Conversation baker in pink, $7-9.

Conversation tidbit in pink, $20-25.

Below:
Conversation plates with decal in pink and gray.

Conversation in brown. These pieces would have been mixed in with coordinating decaled ware.

Conversation shakers in green, $6-8 pr.

Conversation covered sugar in Pebbleford's Marble glaze with leaf decal, $8-10.

Fairway

Produced from the early 1930s until the mid-1940s, Fairway was a decaled and under glaze treatment line. Some colored glazes have been found such as Depression green and the pastel colors used in Lu-Ray. Fairway is usually marked with a general TST backstamp.

Fairway plate in Lu-Ray Pastel's Windsor Blue. UND.

Garland plate and Fairway creamer in Depression green. Plate, $5-7; creamer, 3-4. *Courtesy of Fran & Carl Stone*.

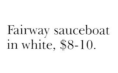

Fairway sauceboat in white, $8-10.

Garland

Like Fairway, Garland was meant for decals and under glaze treatments. However, it was also used in the pink body clay, both plain and with decals. The shape ran from the mid-1930s until early 1953, but the pink body version was used in the 1930s and early 1940s only. The pink clay is the same type developed for the Paramount shape. Garland can be found marked with a general TST backstamp.

Garland plate in pink body clay with clear glaze, $5-7.

Garland covered casserole in black. UND.

Heatherton

Heatherton was made in the 1960s and was sold in single color sets. Four new glazes were developed for Heatherton; egg plant (turquoise), parsley (a sage green glaze), radish (white), and sweet potato (bright yellow).

The flatware is very similar to the Versatile coupe shape, but the hollowware was designed in a formal style. The casserole, sauceboat, sugar and creamer all were modeled with pedestal feet. Lids were made out of wood with brass finials.

Usually, only the larger flatware pieces will carry the Heatherton backstamp.

Heatherton brochure.

Heatherton sugar and creamer in parsley green. Sugar, $5-6; creamer, $3-4.

128

Lu-Ray Pastels

In the late 1930s, many potteries were trying to capitalize on the success of Homer Laughlin's Fiesta. In 1938, Taylor Smith and Taylor took a different approach opting to apply pastel glazes on a streamline form. TST used the newly created Empire shape that was made up of already existing Laurel flatware and specially designed hollowware with low bodies and sweeping handles and finials. The four glazes used were Sharon Pink, Surf Green, Windsor Blue, and Persian Cream.

After it became a hit, other potteries started making their own pastel lines, but none ever attained the level of success TST had with Lu-Ray. TST would go on to use the pastel glazes on the Vogue, Plymouth, and Conversations shapes. Even though they used the exact same glazes as Lu-Ray, they weren't very successful. Lu-Ray Pastels was the perfect match of shape and glaze.

In 1948, TST introduced Chatham Gray. Lu-Ray was sold in rainbow sets of four colors. The idea was to sell sets of basic pieces such as plates, cups and saucers and get buyers to add on by buying the accessory pieces. A fifth color never really worked with this sales concept, and by 1953, gray was discontinued.

By the early 1960s, Lu-Ray had been overshadowed by TST's informal Versatile shape. In 1961, the Lu-Ray Pastels line was discontinued.

Most Lu-Ray can be found today with a backstamp and date code. As the years went on, many pieces were discontinued. By the time gray came out, many shapes were no longer offered. For a full assortment and color availability, see the section on values.

Lu-Ray backstamp.

Lu-Ray plates in the five glazes.

Left: 36s bowls in the four original colors; right: 36s bowls in Chatham Gray. $55-60, gray, $125+.

Lu-Ray teacup and saucer in Persian cream, demitasse cup and saucer in Windsor blue, and chocolate cup and saucer in Sharon pink. *Courtesy of Fran & Carl Stone.*

Shakers in the five Lu-Ray glazes, $20-25; gray, $40-45 pr.

Curved spout teapots in the five Lu-Ray glazes. This style replaced the flat spout version, $85-95; gray, $250+.

Sauceboats in the four original colors, $25-30.

Sauceboat liner/pickle dish in Sharon Pink, $35-40.

The footed jug in Persian Cream was original. It was replaced by the non-footed version as seen in Windsor Blue. With foot, $100-125; no foot, $85-100.

130

Juice pitchers in the four original colors, $125-135.

Juice pitcher in Surf Green with juice tumblers in the four original colors. Pitcher, $125-135; juice tumbler, $70-80.

Lu-Ray Pastels water tumblers and juice tumblers. Tumblers, either style $70-80.

Lu-Ray salad bowls in all five glazes, $65-70; gray, $250+.

Lu-Ray curved spout teapot in Chatham Gray and flat spout teapot in Sharon Pink. Gray teapot $250+, flat spout teapot, $125-145.

Cream soup cup and liner in Persian Cream and lug soup in Chatham Gray. Cream cup and liner, $55-70; lug soup, $50-55.

Right: Lug soup (top) and rim soup (bottom) in Windsor Blue. Lug soup, $18-20; rim soup $15-18. *Courtesy of Fran & Carl Stone*.

Lu-Ray mixing bowls. $200+ each.

Butter dishes in Windsor blue, Sharon pink, and Chatham gray, $65-70; gray, $160+.

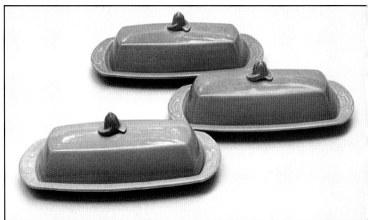

Handleless sugars, $45-50. This shape was more often used with Versatile lines, but some Lu-Ray ads show the handleless sugar offered later in its production.

Covered casserole in Sharon Pink, $90-110.

Double eggcups. $25-30. *Courtesy of Fran & Carl Stone.*

The original demitasse set. These straight-sided pieces were replaced by Empire shapes. Collectors call this older style the "Chocolate Set."

The replacement demitasse set based in the Empire shape.

Lu-Ray nut dishes, $95-110.

Left: Lu-Ray urns, right: Lu-Ray bud vases, $250+ ea.

Lu-Ray epergne in Windsor blue, urn in Sharon pink, bud vase in Persian cream, $250+ ea.

Lu-Ray epergne in Surf green, $250+.

Lu-Ray casserole in Windsor blue with pattern 601 Sterling, $90-110.

Lu-Ray creamer and shakers in Chatham gray with bur-gundy trim. Creamer, $40-45; shakers, $40-45 pr.

Late 1940s Lu-Ray brochure.

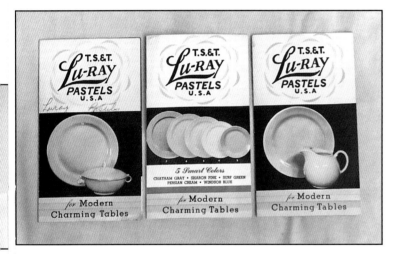

Lu-Ray Pastels brochures.

Leaf Fantasy shape snack set in yellow. TST made these in Persian cream, Surf green, Sharon pink, and Chatham gray. Universal Potteries also made Leaf Fantasy snack sets in their pastel glazes. $15-20 per 2-piece set.

Early 1940s Lu-Ray brochure.

Lu-Ray Pastels fruit cup in pink and soup bowl in gray. The 7" Laurel shape bowl has been found in Surf green and are generally not marked. Fruit cup, $6-8, soup bowl in gray, $40-45, and 7" bowl, UND.

Pebbleford teacups, from left to right: granite, lime (Catalina shape), teal, and mint. $5-8; Catalina, $10-12.

Pebbleford sugars, from left to right: handled base in granite, handle-less base in sand, handle-less in pink, $10-15. *Courtesy of Larisa Self.*

Pebbleford handle-less sugars in turquoise and pink, $10-12.

Catalina shape cups and saucers in the Pebbleford glazes, lime, sunburst, pink, and turquoise, $12-15.

Catalina shape shakers in lime and Versatile shakers in teal. Versatile shakers, $10-12; Castilian, $12-15.

Catalina shakers in Pebbleford pink and Oven-Serve custards in marble. Shakers, $10-12.

Though the specks may not be visible in the photo, all of these pieces have been glazed in sunburst.

Ironstone shape casserole in speckled yellow glaze, $18-20.

Taylor ton "barbeque" mug in turquoise, $10-15. *Courtesy of Larisa Self*.

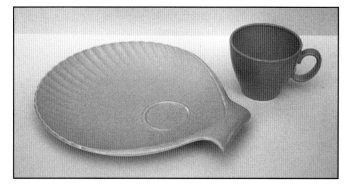

Shell plate and Castilian teacup in Pebbleford pink glaze. Shell plate, $20-25; teacup, $10-12.

Ever Yours shape creamer and sugar in sand. Creamer, $10-12; sugar, $15-18.

French casserole in turquoise and cereal bowl in yellow. French Casserole, $10-15; bowl, $10-15.

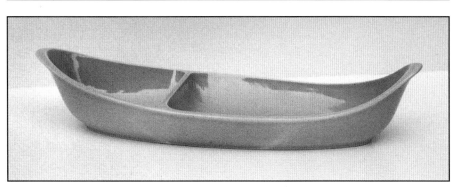

Ever Yours relish in turquoise, $15-18.

Ever Yours carafe in turquoise, $25-30.

Cigarette box in sunburst, $85+. These have also been found in white with decals.

142

NEW!
Mint Green

Pebbleford

VERSATILE FOR MODERN LIVING

Pebbleford's smart, textured pattern and simplicity of design make it right for any occasion. In every setting, from a casual luncheon to a crystal-and-candlelight dinner, the pleasant, soft colors of Pebbleford create harmonious warmth and cheer. In 5 fashion-right, mix-or-match colors: Sunburst, Pink, Turquoise, White, and new Mint Green.

100% CO-OP

OVEN-PROOF AND DETERGENT-PROOF

SUGGESTED RETAIL PRICES

ITEM	EACH	ITEM	EACH	ITEM	EACH	ITEM	EACH
Dinner Plate	$ .80	Cup	.55	Unhandled Covered Sugar	1.15	Chop Plate	2.90
Salad	.60	Saucer	.45	Cream	1.15	Covered Casserole	4.15
Bread and Butter	.50	Vegetable (round)	1.00	Sauceboat	2.00	Covered Butter	1.85
Fruit	.45	Vegetable (Medium)	.95	Pickle	.95	Water Jug	3.40
Lug Soup	.65	11" Platter	1.45	Salt	.70	Divided Baker	2.90
Coupe Soup	.60	13" Platter	2.00	Pepper	.70	16-pc. Starter Set	6.95
		Handled Covered Sugar	1.75	Coffee Server	3.95	53-pc. Dinner Service	25.95

Slightly Higher in the West. Prices subject to change without notice.

Chateau Buffet

IN THE CONTINENTAL TRADITION Chateau Buffet reflects Old World charm and beauty with a graceful contemporary touch. Generous size vessels ideal for entertaining. Timeless in design, modern in serviceability. Chateau Buffet is oven-proof and detergent-proof . . . an ideal gift item!

SUGGESTED RETAIL PRICES

* LE SALADIER (with Fork and Spoon) $9.95
LES ASSIETTES A SALADE (each) .... .75
* LA GRANDE TERRINE (4½ qt.) 9.95
* LA TERRINE MOYENNE (2½ qt.) 8.95
LES RAMEQUINS (each) 1.50
* LA CARAFE 7.95
CUP .... .75
SAUCER .... .50
DINNER PLATE 1.25

Slightly Higher in the West. Prices subject to change without notice.

* Includes Warmer

1963

Plymouth

In 1937, TST introduced the Plymouth shape as its premier dinnerware shape, however, it didn't sell as well as its other lines, Laurel and Empire. Plymouth was made mainly with decals, but there are two instances with solid colors.

The first uses the pink body clay originally designed for Paramount. Pink body Plymouth can be found with and without decals. These pieces, along with decaled white examples, will be marked with the TST wreath backstamp with date code.

The second colored version is a special line which is usually marked, "Interstate Sunrise Ware." This set is made up of the Plymouth shapes in the four Lu-Ray glazes, Windsor Blue, Persian Cream, Sharon Pink, and Surf Green. In rare cases, Interstate Sunrise Ware can be found with decals.

The Plymouth shape was discontinued in the early 1940s.

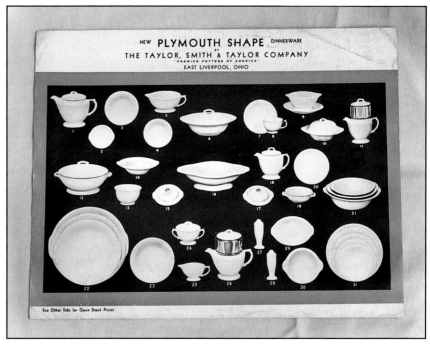

Plymouth promotional card.

Plymouth covered vegetable, demitasse cup and saucer, shaker in pink body with clear glaze. *Courtesy of Fran & Carl Stone.*

Plymouth sugar and creamer in pink body. Sugar, $8-10; creamer, $6-8.

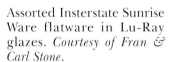

Insterstate Sunrise Ware marking. *Courtesy of Fran & Carl Stone.*

Assorted Insterstate Sunrise Ware flatware in Lu-Ray glazes. *Courtesy of Fran & Carl Stone.*

Left: Insterstate Sunrise Ware cups, saucers, sauceboat and stand, and covered casserole in Lu-Ray glazes. *Courtesy of Fran & Carl Stone.*

Insterstate Sunrise Ware handled tray and 7" plates in Sharon pink with decals and platinum trim.

144

Versatile

Versatile was created in the mid-1950s as a plain round coupe shape. The standard Versatile hollowware is the same that was originally used with Pebbleford. The casual shapes had sweeping handles with no finials or pedestal feet. However, there are many Versatile lines which pick up hollowware from other lines. A popular Versatile line was Dwarf Pine. It had flatware from Versatile, but the hollowware was picked up from the formal shape, Classic. All the pieces were glazed in pink and given the pine decal.

There are also Versatile lines which use the Empire (or Lu-Ray) shapes. In any case, the larger Versatile flatware will be marked, while the smaller flatware and all of the hollowware, regardless of their origin, won't have any backstamp.

Versatile flatware in pastel glazes.

Versatile fruit cups in pastel glazes, $1-2.

Versatile handleless sugars in pink, blue, and green with brown trim, also called "Mint & Spice;" $7-9.

Empire sauceboat and Versatile pickle in yellow with brown trim, also called "Honey & Butter;" $14-18.

145

Mint & Spice gravy, teapot, and shakers. Gravy, $7-9; teapot, $20-25; and shakers, $6-8.

"Cinnamon Stick" cup and saucer, $3-5.

Versatile fruit cups in "Cinnamon Stick" and "Appalachian Plaid," $1-2.

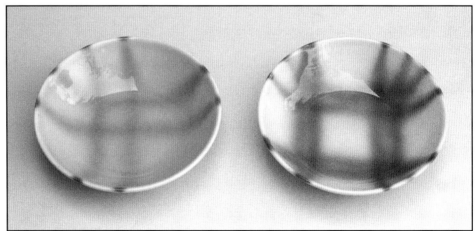

"Appalachian Plaid" sugar and creamer. Sugar, $7-9; creamer, $3-4.

Mint & Spice assortment.

Classic shape casserole in pink, $18-20.

Versatile flatware: "Ming" (yellow) plate and "Dwarf Pine" (pink). The plates have the same decal, but different names depending on the color of the piece.

The Dwarf Pine decal on blue Classic hollowware.

Vistosa

Vistosa was Taylor Smith & Taylor's response to Homer Laughlin's Fiesta. Released in 1938, Vistosa had a more country feel. Rims of flatware and hollowware were modeled with a pie crust type edge. Small daisy flowers adorned the handles on the sugar, creamer, ball jug, and sauceboat as well as the tab handles of the chop plates.

It was offered in red, cobalt, green, and yellow. At least two pieces are known to exist in the Lu-Ray glazes; a ball jug in Windsor Blue and a teacup in Sharon Pink. Several TST decals were used on white Vistosa.

The solid color Vistosa is either marked with a backstamp or raised mold marking. Sometimes pieces are found with their original foil stickers. Decaled Vistosa is almost never marked.

Vistosa was discontinued by 1944.

Vistosa 10" plate in red and 6" plate in green. 10" plates, $45-50; 6", $8-10.

Vistosa cups and saucers, $15-20.

Vistosa lug soup in red, $20-25.

Vistosa 9" plate in cobalt, $15-20.

Vistosa sugar and creamer in yellow. Sugar, $25-30; creamer, $15-20.

Vistosa cup and saucer in cobalt, $15-20.

Vistosa chop plate in green, $35-40.

Vistosa egg cup in red, $45-50.

Vistosa sauceboat in green, $250+.

149

Vistosa sugar and creamer in an odd denim-type glaze, UND.

Vistosa footed salad bowl - original version with scalloped foot, $250+. *Courtesy of Fran & Carl Stone.*

Decaled Vistosa sugar and creamer. Sugar, $25-30; creamer, $15-20

Vistosa footed salad bowl — restyled version with smooth foot, $200-225. *Courtesy of Fran & Carl Stone.*

Vistosa ball jug in red and a rare example in Lu-Ray's Windsor Blue. Jug, standard colors, $85-110.

Decaled Vistosa creamer, $15-20.

Vogue

Vogue was TST's swirl shape of the 1930s and 1940s. The teardrop swirl pattern was crafted on the rims of flatware and on the sides of the bodies of hollowware. The line was meant for decals and under glaze treatments, but after Lu-Ray Pastels became popular in the late 1930s, TST used the pastel glazes on their Vogue shape. The resulting line was called, "Rainbow" and it was sold through Montgomery Wards.

The shakers and ball jug were picked up from the Empire shape. Every other piece in the Rainbow line was from Vogue. None of the pastel glazed Vogue pieces were marked and the line was offered for a limited time.

Vogue advertisement.

Vogue 6" plates in pastel glazes, $2-3.

Vogue fast stands in blue and pink, $10-12.

Vogue fruit cups in the pastel glazes, $2-3.

Vogue cups and saucers in pastel glazes, $5-8.

Vogue platter in green, $10-12.

Vogue sauceboat in blue, $8-10.

Vogue lug soup
in pink, $6-8.

Vogue creamers in
blue and pink, $6-8
ea.

Vogue teapot in
pink, $30-35.

Chapter Eighteen

Universal Potteries, Inc.
Cambridge, Ohio (1934 - 1954)

Universal came into being after several previous reorganizations of potteries (Atlas-Globe, Oxford). Within twenty years, Universal was able to produce massive amounts of dinnerware. Cattail, made as a Sears exclusive, was one of their more popular lines. Of their solid colored lines, Ballerina is the most collected today.

Ballerina

The 1950s line, Ballerina, was made in solid colors, white with decals, and in a blue clay with and without decals. The blue clay version is called Ballerina Mist. The flatware was made up of plain round coupe shapes which became popular in the late 1940s. The hollowware was made round with a slight taper at the foot. The flatware is almost always marked, but the hollowware is often unmarked.

One of the initial Ballerina ads stated: "Ballerina lends itself – blends itself – to reflect your way of life. Your table, set with Ballerina, will captivate your guests at buffets, party-perfect meals, or cozy just-for-two occasions. The shapes are refreshingly modern, but no extreme. Each colored-glaze piece is guaranteed oven-proof - and a complete set stacks away neatly."

Colors include; Forest Green, Chartreuse, Burgundy, Sierra Rust, Jonquil Yellow, Dove Gray, Jade Green, Charcoal, Pink, Turquoise, Periwinkle Blue, and Antique White.

Ballerina sauceboat, creamer and lug soup. Sauceboat, $8-10, creamer, $3-4, and lug soup, $4-6.

Below:
Ballerina shakers in burgundy, $6-8 pr.

Ballerina chop plate in pink, $6-8.

Ballerina tidbit tray in burgundy, $18-20.

Ballerina teapot, demitasse cup and saucer, and water jug. Teapot, $35-40, AD cup and saucer, $12-15, and water jug, $20-25.

Ballerina sugar and creamer. Sugar, $7-9; creamer $3-4.

Ballerina double eggcup, $10-12.

Ballerina demitasse coffeepot in red with white lid, $35-40.

Ballerina covered sugar with pearlized glaze and gold trim, $7-9.

Ballerina Mist handled tray, covered butter, and sauceboat with the Baby's Breath decal treatment. Tray, $6-8; covered butter 10-12; sauceboat, $8-10. *From the collection of Lillian King.*

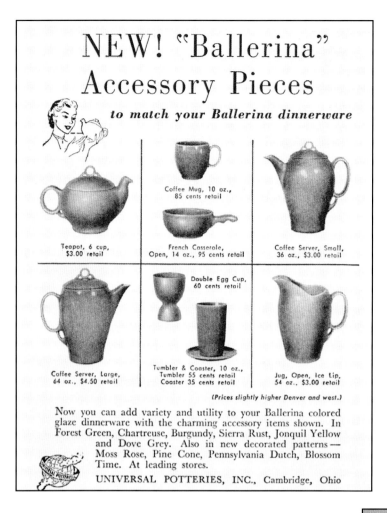
Camwood Ivory

Camwood Ivory was produced during the 1930s through the early 1950s in solid colors and with decals. The four glazes that make up the solid color version are Cocotan (coral), Jade (green), Jonquil (yellow), and Periwinkle (blue). One ad from the 1940s offered Camwood Ivory in the pastel colors as, "Sunny Lane." These same colors were used on the Laurella and Rodeo shapes.

Camwood Ivory is often marked with the circular Universal backstamp along with the shape name.

Camwood Ivory 9" plates, $5-7.

Camwood Ivory cups
and saucers, $5-8.

Camwood Ivory covered casserole, $12-15.

Laurella

Laurella was made in the 1940s and glazed in Universal's solid colors available at the time; Cocotan, Jade, Jonquil, and Periwinkle. (These glazes were also used on Camwood Ivory and Rodeo.) Laurella is one of the few double-duty lines where solid color pieces are easier to find than decaled ones.

Most pieces are marked with the circular Universal mark with Laurella's shape name.

Laruella covered sugar and creamer. Sugar, $7-9; creamer, $3-4.

Rodeo

Rodeo was offered in at least six glazes during the 1940s and early 1950s. The first four are the same used on Camwood Ivory, coral, green, yellow, and blue. The last two were undoubtedly created in the very late 40s or early 50s; gray and chartreuse.

Each piece has the distinctive embossed rope rim. Most pieces are also marked with the Rodeo by Universal backstamp.

In the late 1940s, Montgomery Wards offered Rodeo as, "Bermuda." It wasn't uncommon for a retailer to attach a name to a line of dinnerware. They also renamed the four standard colors as, Sunny Yellow, Turquoise Blue, Apple Green, and Rosy Coral.

Camwood Ivory handled plate, $6-8

Rodeo covered sugar, $7-9.

Camwood Ivory handled tray, $6-8

Sunrise

The Sunrise shape is characterized by its ribbon embossing along the rim. It was made in the standard Universal pastel glazes available in the 1930s and '40s. Sunrise is marked just like the other Universal lines, but unlike its sister shapes, Camwood Ivory and Laurella, it has the Operative Potters marking. This backstamp was used by Universal, Cronin and several others, but doesn't include the Universal name.

Handled tray in yellow, 6-8.

Kitchenware

Universal's kitchenware, Oxford, comes in two styles; with ripples and plain. There were several colors used in Oxford including cobalt, Chinese red, turquoise, yellow, green, blue, and a Fiesta-type red. Pieces may or may bear the Oxford incised marking.

Cobalt and Chinese red are generally applied over a white body so the exteriors are the only parts that have color. All other glazes are applied inside and out.

Oxford teapot in green, $20-25.

Oxford teapot in red, $20-25.
Courtesy of Eva Zia.

Oxford mixing bowls, $10-12. *Courtesy of Eva Zia.*

Tilt top jug pitcher, $20-25.

Range shakers, $8-10. *Courtesy of Eva Zia.*

Universal kitchenware: left to right; ramekin, small bowl, bean pot, and handled tumbler.

Range shakers, $8-10.

Universal teapot. Montgomery Wards sold this color kitchenware as "Aqua," $20-25.

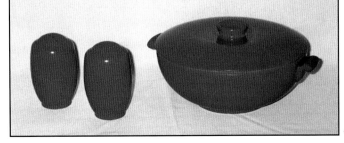

Universal range shakers and covered casserole in a true red glaze. Shakers, $8-10; casserole, $12-15.

Chapter Nineteen

Miscellaneous

Blue/gray body sugar and creamer with clear glaze. Sugar $6-8; creamer $3-4.

Embossed square plate in green, $8-10.

Hall China "Gaco" mixing bowl in red, $25-30.

Salem China promotional plates, $30-35.

Cake set in green, $25-35.

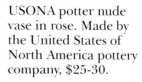

USONA potter nude vase in rose. Made by the United States of North America pottery company, $25-30.

Bibliography

Duke, Harvey. *The Official Price Guide to Pottery and Porcelain, 8th edition*. New York, New York: House of Collectibles, 1995.

Gonzalez, Mark. *An Overview of Homer Laughlin Dinnerware*. Gas City, Indiana: L-W Book Sales, 2002.

Gonzalez, Mark. *Collecting Fiesta, Lu-Ray and Other Colorware*. Gas City, Indiana: L-W Book Sales, 2000.

Meehan, Kathy and Bill. *Collector's Guide to Lu-Ray Pastels*. Paducah, Kentucky: Collector Books, 1995.

Sanford, Martha & Steve. *Sanfords Guide to McCoy Pottery*. San Jose, California: Adelmore Press, 1997.

Spargo, John. *Early American Pottery and China*. New York, New York: The Century Co., 1926.

Stiles, Helen E. *Pottery in the United States*. New York, New York: E.P. Dutton & Co., Inc., 1941.

Whitmyer, Margaret and Ken. *The Collector's Encyclopedia of Hall China, 2nd edition*. Paducah, Kentucky: Collector Books, 1997.

Values

Old Holland

10" plate	$6-8
9" plate	$5-7
7" plate	$4-6
6" plate	$3-4
Teacup	$4-6
Tea saucer	$1-2
Creamer	$3-4
Sugar	$7-9
Covered casserole	$12-15
Sauceboat	$8-10
13" platter	$8-10
11" platter	$6-8
5" Fruit cup	$1-2
6" Oatmeal	$2-3
Rim soup	$4-6
Lug soup	$4-6
Nappy	$5-7
Oval baker	$5-7

Zephyr

10" plate	$6-8
9" plate	$5-7
7" plate	$4-6
6" plate	$3-4
Teacup	$4-6
Tea saucer	$1-2
Creamer, any style	$3-4
Sugar, any style	$7-9
Tab-handled plate, any style	$8-10
5" Fruit cup	$1-2
6" Oatmeal	$2-3
Soup	$4-6
Nappy	$5-7
Shakers	$6-8
Pie plate	$8-10

Romany & Ranchero

10" plate	$6-8
9" plate	$5-7
7" plate	$4-6
6" plate	$3-4
Teacup	$4-6
Tea saucer	$1-2
Creamer	$3-4
Sugar, covered	$7-9
Covered casserole	$20-25
Covered vegetable	$12-15
Sauceboat	$8-10
11" round platter	$6-8

Basketweave

5" Fruit cup	$1-2
6" Oatmeal	$2-3
Rim soup	$4-6
Lug soup	$4-6
Nappy	$5-7
Shakers, short, pr.	$8-10
Shakers, tall, pr.	$8-10

10" plate	$6-8
9" plate	$5-7
7" plate	$4-6
6" plate	$2-3
11" platter	$6-8
9" platter	$4-5
Divided plate	$6-8
Batter jug	$15-20
Syrup jug	$10-12
Teacup	$3-4
Saucer	$1
Creamer	$4-5
Covered sugar	$5-6
Gravy	$6-8
Double eggcup	$8-10
5" fruit cup	$2-3
6" oatmeal	$3-4
Soup bowl	$4-5
Nappy	$5-6
Oval baker	$5-6
Teapot	$25-35
Covered casserole	$12-15

Bolero

10" plate	$6-8
9" plate	$4-5
8" plate	$4-5
6" plate	$2-3
Teacup	$2-3
Saucer	$1
Creamer, with lid	$6-8
Restyled creamer	$4-5
Covered sugar	$8-10
Restyled sugar	$5-7
Compote	$18-20
Casseroles:	
Regular	$18-20
Straight sided	$20-25
Oval teapot	$35-40
Round teapot	$35-40
Shell dish	$8-10
12" chop plate	$8-10
11" oval platter	$6-8

Elmhurst

Pickle	$5-7
Gravy, double lip	$10-12
Lug dish	$5-7
Custard	$3-4
Cream soup cup with lid	$12-15
10" lug salad bowl	$6-8
6" lug soup	$3-5
9" oval baker	$6-7
9" round nappy	$6-7
Fruit cup	$2-3
Oatmeal	$3-4

10" plate	$6-8
9" plate	$5-7
7" plate	$4-6
6" plate	$3-4
Teacup	$4-6
Tea saucer	$1-2
Creamer	$3-4
Sugar, covered	$7-9
Covered casserole	$20-25
Double egg cup	$8-10
Sauceboat	$8-10
Gravy fast stand	$15-18
15" platter	$10-12
13" platter	$8-10
11" platter	$6-8
9" platter	$6-8
36s bowl	$8-10
5" Fruit cup	$1-2
6" Oatmeal	$2-3
Coupe soup	$4-6
Lug soup	$4-6
Nappy	$5-7
9" oval baker	$5-7
Teapot	$30-35

Fifties Lines

10" plate	$6-8
9" plate	$5-7
7" plate	$4-6
6" plate	$3-4
Teacup	$4-6
Tea saucer	$1-2
Creamer	$3-4
Sugar, covered	$7-9
Covered casserole	$12-15
Covered butter	$8-10
Teapot	$15-18
Sauceboat	$8-10

13" platter	$8-10
11" platter	$6-8
5" Fruit cup	$1-2
6" Oatmeal	$2-3
Rim soup	$4-6
Lug soup	$4-6
Nappy	$5-7
Oval baker	$5-7
Divided baker	$8-10

Geometric

10" plate	$6-8
9" plate	$5-7
7" plate	$4-6
6" plate	$3-4
Teacup	$4-6
Tea saucer	$1-2
Creamer	$3-4
Sugar, covered	$8-10
Covered casserole	$20-25
Teapot	$25-30
Sauceboat	$8-10
13" platter	$8-10
11" platter	$6-8
5" Fruit cup	$1-2
6" Oatmeal	$2-3
Rim soup	$4-6
Lug soup	$4-6
Nappy	$5-7
9" oval baker	$5-7

Georgette / Petal

10" plate	$6-8
9" plate	$5-7
7" plate	$4-6
6" plate	$3-4
Teacup	$4-6
Tea saucer	$1-2
Creamer	$3-4
Sugar, covered	$7-9
Teapot	$30-35
Covered casserole	$12-15
Sauceboat	$8-10
13" platter	$8-10
11" platter	$6-8
9" platter	$5-7
5" Fruit cup	$1-2
6" Oatmeal	$2-3
Rim soup	$4-6
Lug soup	$4-6
Nappy	$5-7
9" oval baker	$5-7
10" oval baker	$6-8
36s bowl	$6-8
Jumbo cup	$6-8
Jumbo saucer	$1-2
Shakers, pr.	$8-10

Rainbow and Petit-point

10" plate	$6-8
9" plate	$5-7
7" plate	$4-6
6" plate	$3-4
Teacup	$4-6
Tea saucer	$1-2
Creamer	$3-4

Double eggcup	$10-12
Sugar, covered	$7-9
Covered casserole	$18-20
Sauceboat	$8-10
13" platter	$8-10
11" platter	$6-8
9" platter	$6-8
5" Fruit cup	$1-2
6" Oatmeal	$2-3
Rim soup	$4-6
Lug soup	$4-6
Nappy	$5-7
Oval baker	$5-7

Accent

6" plate	$1
8" plate	$1
10" plate	$2-3
Coffeepot	$10-15
10" round vegetable	$3-4
Lug soup	$2-3
vegetable:	
10" round cover	$6-8
8" round cover	$8-10
Creamer	$2-3
Covered sugar	$3-4
Shakers, pr.	$6-8
8" nappy	$2-3
Sauceboat	$4-5
Fruit cup	$1
Coupe soup	$2-3
Pickle	$2-3
15" platter	$5-6
13" platter	$3-4
Teacup	$1-2
Saucer	$1
Snack plate	$5-6
Tid-bit	$7-9

Cameo

10" plate	$6-8
9" plate	$5-7
7" plate	$4-6
6" plate	$3-4
Teacup	$4-6
Tea saucer	$1-2
Creamer	$5-7
Sugar	$10-12
Covered casserole	$18-20
Sauceboat	$8-10
13" platter	$8-10
11" platter	$6-8
5" Fruit cup	$1-2
6" Oatmeal	$2-3
Rim soup	$4-6
Lug soup	$4-6
Nappy	$5-7
Oval baker	$5-7

Creme Flute

10" plate	$8-10
9" plate	$5-6
7" plate	$3-4
6" plate	$2-3
Covered casserole	$18-20
Covered sugar	$8-10

Creamer	$5-7
Sauceboat	$6-8
Oval baker	$5-7
36s bowl	$10-12
13" platter	$8-10
11" platter	$7-8
9" platter	$6-8
7" platter	$6-8
Egg cup	$10-12
5" fruit cup	$2-3
6" fruit cup	$3-4
Round nappy	$5-6
Tea cup	$3-4
Saucer	$1

Deanna

AD coffee	$8-10
AD saucer	$1-2
9" oval baker	$5-6
36s bowl	$8-10
Round open butter	$10-12
Covered casserole	$40-45
Chop plate	$8-10
Coaster	$6-8
Coupe soup	$5-6
Creamer	$5-6
11" platter	$8-10
13" platter	$8-10
15" platter	$10-12
Double egg cup	$12-15
5" fruit cup	$3-4
6" oatmeal bowl	$4-5
Lug soup	$6-8
9" nappy	$5-6
10" nappy	$6-8
Shakers, pair	$12-15
Relish/pickle	$6-8
10" plate	$6-8
9" plate	$5-6
8" plate	$8-10
7" plate	$5-6
6" plate	$3-4
Sauceboat	$8-10
Covered sugar	$6-8
Teacup, any style	$4-5
Saucer	$1
Teapot	$35-40

Marion

10" plate	$6-8
9" plate	$5-7
7" plate	$4-6
6" plate	$3-4
Teacup	$4-6
Tea saucer	$1-2
Creamer	$3-4
Sugar, covered	$7-9
Covered casserole	$18-20
Sauceboat	$8-10
13" platter	$8-10
11" platter	$6-8
5" Fruit cup	$1-2
6" Oatmeal	$2-3
Rim soup	$4-6
Lug soup	$4-6
Nappy	$5-7
9" oval baker	$5-7

10" oval baker	$6-8
Covered batter jug	$15-20
Covered syrup jug	$10-12
Divided child's dish	$12-15

Maryland

10" baker	$6-8
9" baker	$6-8
9" bread plate	$6-8
36s bowl	$8-10
8-oz. Bouillon cups	$6-8
Bouillon saucer	$2-3
Covered butter	$8-10
Demitasse cup	$6-8
Demitasse saucer	$2-3
Covered jugs:	
¾-pt.	$8-10
1-pt.	$12-15
2 ¾- pt.	$18-20
Creamer	$3-5
Cream soup cup	$5-7
Cream soup liner	$2-3
11" platter	$8-10
13" platter	$10-12
15" platter	$15-18
17" platter	$20-25
Double eggcup	$10-12
5" fruit cup	$2-3
1 ½-pt. Jug	$15-18
3 ¼-pt. Jug	$20-25
8" nappy	$5-7
9" nappy	$5-7
10" nappy	$6-8
6" oatmeal	$3-4
9" pickle	$6-8
6" plate	$2-3
7" plate	$3-5
8" plate	$5-7
9" plate	$6-8
10" plate	$10-12
8" coupe soup	$5-7
Sauceboats:	
regular	$10-12
fast stand	$10-12
Covered sugar	$6-8
Teapot	$35-40
Tea cup	$5-6
Tea saucer	$1

Plaid

10" plate	$6-8
9" plate	$5-7
7" plate	$4-6
6" plate	$3-4
Teacup	$4-6
Tea saucer	$1-2
Creamer	$3-4
Sugar	$7-9
Covered casserole	$20-25
Sauceboat	$8-10
13" platter	$6-8
11" platter	$6-8
5" Fruit cup	$1-2
6" Oatmeal	$2-3
Rim soup	$4-6
Lug soup	$4-6
Nappy	$5-7

Oval baker	$5-7

Potomac

Lug soup	$1-2
Pickle dish	$3-5
Round open butter	$5-6
36s bowl	$5-6
Shakers, pr	$6-8
Cream soup cup	$3-4
Cream soup liner	$1-2
Rim soup	$3-4
5" fruit cup	$2-3
6" oatmeal bowl	$3-4
Tea cup	$3-4
Saucer	$1
AD cup	$5-6
AD saucer	$1-2
6" plate	$1-2
7" plate	$2-3
8" plate	$6-8
9" plate	$5-7
10" plate	$6-8
Square plate	$6-8
12" chop plate	$6-8
Creamer	$3-4
Coffeepot	$10-15
Sugar	$5-6
8" baker	$3-4
9" baker	$3-4
Sauceboat	$5-6
Casserole	$10-15
7" platter	$3-4
9" platter	$3-4
11" platter	$5-7
13" platter	$5-7
8" nappy	$3-4
9" nappy	$3-4
10" nappy	$4-5

Utility Ware

6" mixing bowl	$8-10
8" mixing bowl	$12-15
10" mixing bowl	$15-18
9" round salad bowl	$18-20
Cake server	$15-18
Spoon	$15-18
Fork	$15-18
1 ½ pt. Jug	$20-25
2 ½ pt. Jug	$20-25
3 pt. Jug	$25-30
4 ½ pt. Jug	$30-35
Cookie Jar	$40-50
Utility plate	$8-10
8" casserole	$20-25
7" casserole	$20-25
Covered butter	$30-35
Custard cup	$5-8
Pie plate	$12-15
4" round leftover	$8-10
5" round leftover	$10-12
6" round leftover	$15-18
Teapot	$40-50
Batter set tray	$12-15
Shirred egg	$10-12
Range shakers, pr.	$12-15
Mug	$18-20

Yorktown

36s bowl	$10-12
Round open butter	$12-15
Candlesticks, pair	$80-95
Covered casserole	$35-40
Coaster	$10-12
AD coffee	$10-12
AD saucer	$3-5
Fruit Console bowl	$18-20
Creamer	$8-10
Custard cup/ramekin	$8-10
11" round platter	$10-12
13" round platter	$10-12
15" round platter	$12-15
Fruit cup	$5-6
8" nappy	$8-10
9" nappy	$8-10
10" nappy	$8-10
Oatmeal bowl	$6-8
6" plate	$3-4
7" plate	$4-5
8" plate	$8-10
9" plate	$6-8
10" plate	$8-10
Coupe soup	$7-9
Lug soup	$8-10
Pickle dish	$7-9
Shakers, pair	$12-15
Sauceboats:	
two handles	$15-18
one handle	$12-15
Covered sugar	$12-15
Teacup	$6-8
Saucer	$1-2
Teapot	$40-45

"Lotus"

10" plate	$6-8
9" plate	$5-7
7" plate	$4-6
6" plate	$3-4
Teacup	$4-6
Tea saucer	$1
Creamer	$3-4
AD cup	$6-8
AD saucer	$1-2
Sugar, covered	$7-9
Covered casserole	$12-15
Sauceboat	$8-10
13" platter	$8-10
11" platter	$6-8
5" Fruit cup	$1-2
6" Oatmeal	$2-3
Coupe soup	$4-6
Lug soup	$4-6
Nappy	$5-7
9" oval baker	$5-7
10" oval baker	$6-8
36s bowl	$6-8
Covered batter jug	$25-30
Covered syrup jug	$20-25

Antique Orleans

10" plate	$8-10
9" plate	$7-9
8" plate	$10-12

167

167

7" plate $5-6
6" plate $2-3
Teacup $6-8
Tea saucer $2-3
Creamer $6-8
Sugar, open $10-15
Sugar, covered $15-20
Covered casserole $40-45
Sauceboat $12-15
13" platter $10-12
11" platter $10-12
15" platter $12-15
5" Fruit cup $2-3
6" Oatmeal $5-6
Rim soup $8-10
10" Nappy $10-12
9" Nappy $10-12
9" oval baker $8-10
10" oval baker $8-10
Pickle dish $8-10
36s bowl $10-12
Jug $30-35

Carnival

6" plate $3-4
Fruit cup $3-4
Oatmeal bowl $3-4
Teacup $5-6
Saucer $1

Colorama

Plates, any size $2-3
Platters, any size $3-4
Creamer $2-3
Covered sugar $3-5
Casserole $8-10
Teacup $2-3
Saucer $1
Sauceboat $3-5

Coronet

10" plate $12-14
9" plate $8-10
7" plate $5-7
6" plate $4-5
Teacup $7-9
Tea saucer $2-3
Creamer $7-9
Sugar, open $15-18
Sugar, covered $18-20
Covered casserole $45-50
Sauceboat $10-12
Sauceboat liner $10-12
15" platter $18-20
13" platter $12-15
11" platter $8-10
5" Fruit cup $4-5
6" Oatmeal $6-8
36s bowl $10-12
Rim soup $8-10
Coupe soup $10-12
Lug soup $12-15
Nappy $10-12
Oval baker $8-10

Dover

Chop plate $5-6
10" plate $3-4
7" plate $1-2
6" plate $1
Coffeepot $15-18
Covered sugar $5-6
Creamer $3-4
Nappy $3-4
Teacup $1-2
Saucer $1
Shakers $3-4 pr.
Sauceboat $5-6
Covered Butter $6-7

Teapot $15-18
Large salad bowl $10-12
Covered casserole $12-15
Tureen $18-20
Ladle $4-5
Lug soup $1-2
Soup bowl $3-4
Fruit cup $1-2
Platter $4-5
Sauceboat liner $3-4

Epicure

Ashtray UND
9" nappy salad bowl $18-20
Coupe soup $15-18
Covered casserole $70-80
Individual casserole $50-60
Coffeepot $200+
Creamer $10-12
Coffee cup $12-15
Coffee saucer $5-6
Cereal dish $18-20
Fruit dish $8-10
Nut dish $30-35
Gravy $25-30
Gravy liner $25-30
Ladle $60-70
6" plate $4-5
8" plate $15-18
10" plate $18-20
9" oval platter $30-35
11" oval platter $18-20
Shakers, pair $20-25
Covered sugar $18-20
Tidbit tray $65-70

Fiesta

NA = Not available.
50s colors = rose, gray, dark green, chartreuse.

	Red, Cobalt Ivory	Lt. green Turquoise Yellow	50s colors	Medium green
Ashtray	$50-60	$35-40	$75-90	$120+
Bowl covered onion soup	$400-450	$325-350 (1,000+ turquoise)	NA	NA
Bowls:				
cream soup	$65-85	$30-35	$75-95	$3,000
6" dessert	$50-60	$25-35	$80+	$500+
footed-salad	$250-275	$185-200	NA	NA
Fruit bowls:				
11.75"	$250-275	$185-200	NA	NA
5 1/2"	$25-30	$20-25	$45-50	$85-90
4 3/4"	$25-30	$25-35	$35-40	$650+
Mixing Bowls:				
#1	$225-250	$220-240	NA	NA
#2	$95-100	$85-95	NA	NA
#3	$110-125	$110-115	NA	NA

	Red, Cobalt Ivory	Lt. green Turquoise Yellow	50s colors	Medium green
#4	$130-145	$120-135	NA	NA
#5	$150-165	$130-140	NA	NA
#6	$175-200	$140-160	NA	NA
#7	$250+	$200-225	NA	NA
Mixing Bowl Lids:				
#5	UND	UND	NA	NA
#6	UND	UND	NA	NA
Nappy Bowls				
9 1/2"	$55-60	$45-50	NA	NA
8 1/2"	$45-55	$25-35	$60-70	$150+
Candle-holders:				
bulb, pr.	$100-115	$90-95	NA	NA
tripod	$450-600	$350-500	NA	NA
Carafe	$200-250	$125-175	NA	NA
Casserole	$200-225	$125-150	$200-250	$900+
Coffeepot	$200-250	$150-175	$300-325	NA
Coffeepot Demitasse	$550-600	$400-450	NA	NA
Comport 12"	$185-200	$85-95	NA	NA

	Red, Cobalt Ivory	Lt. green Turquoise Yellow	50s colors	Medium green
Comport sweets	$100-125	$85-95	NA	NA
Creamer	$20-25	$15-20	$40-45	$75-85
Creamer stick-handled	$55-60	$45-50 ($75 turquoise)	NA	NA
Teacup	$25-35	$18-20	$40-45	$65-75
Saucer	$4-5	$2-3	$5-7	$10-15
AD Cup	$45-50	$35-40	$200-250	UND
AD saucer	$15-18	$12-15	$50-60	UND
Cup egg	$75-85	$35-45	$100-125	UND
Marmalade	$250-275	$180-225	NA	NA
Mug				
Tom & Jerry	$75-80	$45-50	$85-95	$95-115
Mustard	$250-275	$180-225	NA	NA
Pitchers:				
disk water	$140-150	$95-100	$225-250	$1500+
ice-lip	$150-175	$115-135	NA	NA
2-pt jug	$80-100	$60-75	$130+	NA
Plates:				
cake	$350, any color			NA
NA				
13" Chop	$35-40	$20-25	$45-55	$100+
15" Chop	$55-60	$40-45	$75-85	NA
12" Chop	$55-60	$45-50 (no turquoise)	NA	NA
10 1/2"	$45-50	$35-45	$70-75	NA
8" deep	$40-45	$35-40	$45-50	$95-100
10"	$50-60	$35-45	$70-80	$125+
9"	$30-35	$15-20	$35-40	$85-90
7"	$10-15	$8-10	$15-20	$45-50
6"	$8-10	$6-8	$10-12	$30-35
Platter	$40-50	$35-40	$55-60	$150+
Shakers S/P	$35-40	$25-30	$35-40	$85-100
Sauce Boat	$55-65	$25-30	$75-85	$150-175
Sugar Bowl				
with Lid	$300-325	$250-275	NA	NA
Syrup	$300-350	$275-300	NA	NA
Lg. Teapot	$250-260	$185-200	NA	NA
Med. teapot	$250-300	$200-225	$300-325	$1,500+
Tray relish				
with inserts	$300-350	NA	NA	NA
Tray utility	$40-50	$35-40	NA	NA
Tumbler water	$70-75	$40-45	NA	NA
Vase 12"	$1000	$850-900	NA	NA
Vase 10"	$800-900	$750-800	NA	NA
Vase 8"	$650-700	$450-500	NA	NA
Vase bud	$85-95	$75-85	NA	NA
Mixing Bowl				
with Lids, #1-4	$400+	$400+	NA	NA
Salad Bowl,				
unlisted	NA	$100-120	NA	NA
Tray figure-8	$65-70	$200+	NA	NA
Ind. Sugar Bowl	NA	$85-100	NA	NA
Ind. Creamer	NA	$55-65	NA	NA
Casserole, French	NA	$150-175	NA	NA
Pitcher disk juice	$250	$40-50	NA	NA
Tumbler juice	$40-45	$20-25	NA	$20-25

See sections on Rhythm and Jubilee for more.

Harlequin

	Red, maroon, Spruce green	Lt. green mauve blue, rose, yellow turquoise	50s colors	Medium green
10" Plate	$20-25	$18-20	$30-35	$50-55
9" Plate	$15-18	$10-12	$18-20	$40-45
7" Plate	$8-10	$7-9	$12-15	$15-20
6" Plate	$6-8	$7-9	$12-15	$15-20
13" Platter	$20-25	$15-18	$25-30	$150
11" Platter	$18-20	$12-15	$25-30	$150
Sugar	$30-35	$20-25	$35-40	$125
Creamers:				
Regular	$10-12	$7-9	$15-18	$60-70
Novelty	$20-25	$12-15	$30-35	$1200
Teacup	$10-12	$8-10	$12-15	$20-25
Saucer	$3-5	$1-2	$6-8	$12-15
Sauceboat	$18-20	$12-15	$25-30	$175
Shakers, pr.	$15-20	$15-20	$30-35	$200
Fruit Cup	$10-12	$8-10	$15-18	$20-25
Oatmeal	$18-20	$12-15	$25-30	$35-40
36s bowl	$30-35	$20-25	$40-45	$125+
Nappy	$18-20	$15-18	$30-35	$100+
7 3/8" salad	$20-25	$15-18	$30-35	$85+
AD Cup	$45-50	$35-40	$100	$300
AD saucer	$12-15	$8-10	$18-20	$60-75
Cream Soup Cup	$20-25	$15-20	$50-65	$850+
Rim soup	$18-20	$12-15	$40-45	$95-110
22oz. Jug	$60-75	$40-50	$60-75	$500+
Ball Jug	$70-80	$35-45	$125+	$1800+
Teapot	$150-175	$110-125	$200+	$500+
Casserole	$95-110	$75-85	$150+	$500+
Basketweave				
ashtray	$30-35	$20-25	$100+	$250+
Double eggcup	$18-20	$12-15	$30-35	$200+

	Maroon, red, Spruce gr.	mauve blue, rose, yellow turquoise	light green
Regular ashtray	$50-60	$40-45	$65+
saucer ashtray	$60-75	$50-55	$75+
Ind. creamer	$20-25	$18-20	$75+
Baker	$20-25	$12-15	$30-35
Single eggcup	$25-30	$18-20	$100+
Marmalade	$200-225	$150-180	$350+
Nut dish	$20-25	$18-20	$75+
Pr, candleholders	$300+	$350+	$UND
Butter (Jade shape)	$125-135	$95-110	$95-110
Tumbler	$35-40	$25-30	$25-30

	maroon spruce	mauve, yellow rose, turquoise	any colors
High lip creamer	$120-$145	$120-145	NA
Relish tray	NA	$250-275	$250+
Syrup	$350	$350	$350
Jumbo cup	NA	$300+	$300+
Jumbo saucer	NA	$75+	$75+

Shakers, pair	$6-8		5" Fruit cup	$1-2		Lug cake plate	$7-9
Oval baker	$7-9		6" Oatmeal	$2-3		5" fruit cup	$1-2
Nappy	$7-9		Rim soup	$4-6		6" oatmeal	$3-4
Covered casserole	$10-12		Lug soup	$4-6		Rim soup	$6-8
Service jug	$15-18		Nappy	$5-7			
Coffeepot	$15-18		9" oval baker	$5-7			
13" platter	$8-10		10" oval baker	$6-8			

Heatherton

11" platter	$6-8
Sauceboat	$8-10
Sauceboat stand	$7-9
Tid-bit	$20-25

Garland

10" plate	$5-7
7" plate	$4-6
6" plate	$3-4
Teacup	$4-6
Tea saucer	$1-2
Creamer	$3-4
Sugar, covered	$5-6
Covered casserole	$12-15
Sauceboat	$5-6
Sauceboat liner	$3-5
Coffeepot	$15-20
13" platter	$5-7
11" platter	$5-7
5" Fruit cup	$1-2
6" Oatmeal	$2-3
Rim soup	$4-6
Lug soup	$4-6
Nappy	$5-7

Fairway

			10" plate	$6-8
			9" plate	$5-7
10" plate	$6-8		7" plate	$4-6
9" plate	$5-7		6" plate	$3-4
7" plate	$4-6		Teacup	$3-4
6" plate	$3-4		Tea saucer	$1-2
Teacup	$4-6		Teapot	$20-25
Tea saucer	$1-2		Covered casserole	$18-20
Creamer	$3-4		Covered sugar	$8-10
Sugar, open	$7-9		Creamer	$5-6
Sugar, covered	$7-9		Baker	$6-8
Covered casserole	$12-15		Nappy	$6-8
Sauceboat	$8-10		Covered nappy	$10-12
13" platter	$8-10		13" platter	$8-10
11" platter	$6-8		11" platter	$6-8
			Sauceboat	$8-10
			Pickle, sauceboat stand	$4-6

Lu-Ray Pastels

	Approx. Dates of Production	Four orig. Colors	Chatham Gray		Approx. Dates of Production	Four orig. Colors	Chatham Gray
Plates:							
10"	1938-1961	$20-25	$30-35	Double eggcup	1939-1955	$25-30	$80-85
9"	1938-1961	$12-15	$20-25	Lug soup	1938-1955	$18-20	$50-55
8"	1938-1961	$20-25	$45-50	**Cream soup:**			
7"	1938-1961	$9-12	$20-25	cup	1938-1945	$45-50	NA
6"	1938-1961	$7-9	$15-20	liner	1938-1945	$18-20	NA
Chop	1938-1955	$40-50	$275+	Covered butter			
Compartment	1941-1955	$30-35	$100-125	dish	1941-1955	$65-70	$160+
Teacup	1938-1961	$8-10	$25-30	Salad bowl	1941-1945	$65-70	$250+
Tea saucer	1938-1961	$3-4	$8-10	**Jugs:**			
Demitasse cup	1940-1955	$25-30	$40-45	footed	1938-1941	$100-125	NA
saucer	1940-1955	$12-15	$15-18	no foot	1941-1955	$85-100+	NA
Chocolate cup	1939-1940	$100+	NA	**Juice:**			
Choc. saucer	1939-1940	$50-55	NA	pitcher	1941-1945	$125-135	NA
Creamers:				tumbler	1941-1945	$70-80	NA
regular	1938-1961	$10-12	$40-45	Water tumbler	1942-1945	$70-80	NA
demitasse	1939-1940	$45-50	NA	Muffin cover	1940-1945	$90-100	NA
chocolate	1940-1945	$300+	NA	Gravy faststand	1938-1955	$40-45	NA
Sugars:				Gravy Sauceboat	1938-1945	$25-30	NA
regular	1938-1955	$22-25	$75-85	Demitasse			
demitasse	1940-1945	$65-75	NA	pot	1940-1945	$185-200	NA
chocolate	1939-1940	$400+	NA	Chocolate pot	1939-1940	$650+	NA
no handles	1955 - 1961	$45-50	NA	Handled cake			
Teapot:				plate	1938-1945	$65-75	NA
flat spout	1938-1941	$125-145	NA	Shakers, pr.	1938-1961	$20-25	$40-45
curved spout	1941-1955	$85-95	$250+	4-part relish	1938-1942	$95-100	NA
Covered casserole	1938-1945	$90-110	NA	**Mixing bowls:**			
Nappy	1938-1961	$18-20	$45-50	10"	1941-1942	$200+	NA
Baker	1938-1961	$18-20	$45-55	8"	1941-1942	$200+	NA
Fruit cup	1938-1961	$6-8	$30-35	7"	1941-1942	$200+	NA
36s bowl	1938-1955	$55-60	$125+	5"	1941-1942	$200+	NA
Rim soup	1938-1961	$15-18	$40-45	**Flower Vase:**			
Platters:				Epergne	1939-1942	$250+	NA
13"	1938-1961	$20-22	$40-45	Bud urn	1939-1942	$250+	NA
11"	1938-1961	$20-22	$40-45	Bud vase	1939-1942	$250+	NA
Pickle/sauceboat				Nut dish/coaster	1942-1945	$95-110	NA
stand	1938-1945	$35-40	NA				

Paramount and Regal

10" plate	$7-9
9" plate	$6-8
8" plate	$7-9
7" plate	$5-6
6" plate	$4-5
Fruit cup	$3-4
Oatmeal bowl	$4-5
36s bowl	$10-12
Rim soup	$6-8
Cream soup cup	$6-8
Cream soup liner	$3-4
Compartment plate	$10-12
Handled tray w/ well	$12-15
Handled tray w/o well	$10-12
17" platter	$12-15
15" platter	$10-12
13" platter	$8-10
11" platter	$8-10
9" platter	$6-8
Pickle	$5-6
Cover, 11" platter	$12-15
Batter jug	$20-25
Syrup pitcher	$18-20
Sauceboat	$8-10
Gravy fast-stand	$10-12
Creamer	$4-6
Sugar	$5-8
Teacup, tall	$4-6
Teacup, short	$4-6
Saucer	$1-2
Covered casserole	$20-25
Teapot	$30-35
Muffin cover	$20-25
Butter dish	$12-15
10" nappy	$6-8
9" nappy	$5-7
10" baker	$6-8
9" baker	$5-7

Pebbleford

12" chop plate	$15-18
10" plate	$10-12
7" plate	$6-8
6" plate	$4-6
11" platter	$10-12
13" platter	$12-15
Teacup, regular	$5-8
Teacup, Empire	$15-18
Teacup, Catalina	$10-12
Saucer	$2-3
Sugar with handles	$12-15
Sugar without handles	$10-12
Empire	$18-20
Ever Yours	$15-18
Creamers, regular	$6-8
Creamer, empire	$12-15
Creamer, catalina	$10-12
Ever Yours	$10-12
Sauceboat	$12-15
Shakers, regular	$10-12
Shakers, Catalina	$12-15
Covered casserole	$18-20
Divided baker	$15-18
Oval vegetable	$10-12
Round serving bowl	$10-12
Coupe soup	$8-10

Pickle	$9-12
Fruit cup	$4-6
10" mixing bowl	$100+
8" mixing bowl	$100+
7" mixing bowl	$100+
5" mixing bowl	$100+
Lug soup	$8-10
Lug soup lid	$15-18
Egg cup	$15-20
Covered butter dishes:	
with finial	$18-20
without finial	$20-25
Empire shape	$30-35
Covered cheese dish	$55-65
Water jug	$35-40
Teapot	$40-45
Coffee pots:	
3" opening	$30-35
4" opening	$30-35
Classic	$40-45
Covered cigarette box	$85+
Cake lifter	$20-25
Coffee carafe, Ever Yours	$25-30
Flared bowl	$8-10
Relish, Ever Yours	$15-18
Shell snack plate	$20-25
Taylor barbeque mug	$10-15
Chateau Buffet Bowl	$10-15
Small French casserole	$10-15
Therma-Role	$300+
Cookie jar	$250+
Canister, first size	UND
Canister, second size	UND
Canister, third size	UND
Canister, fourth size	UND

Plymouth

Teapot, 6-cup	$25-30
Teapot, 8-cup	$25-30
10" plate	$7-9
9" plate	$6-8
8" plate	$7-9
7" plate	$5-7
6" plate	$3-4
Lug soup	$4-6
Covered vegetable	$10-12
Covered casserole	$20-25
Console bowl	$25-30
Candleholders, pr	$20-25
Shakers, pr	$10-12
Sauceboat	$8-10
Sugar	$8-10
Creamer	$6-8
Pickle	$6-8
Fast-stand	$10-12
Cream soup cup	$10-12
Cream soup liner	$4-6
Covered butter, round	$18-20
Teacup	$4-6
Tea saucer	$1-2
Demitasse cup	$6-8
Demitasse saucer	$2-3
36s bowl	$8-10
Soup bowl	$5-7
Oatmeal bowl	$4-6
Fruit cup	$3-4
Coaster	$10-12
8" nappy	$6-8

9" nappy	$6-8
10" nappy	$7-9
Baker	$10-12
11" lug chop plate	$10-12
13" lug chop plate	$12-15
15" lug chop plate	$15-18

Versatile

Teacup	$2-3
Saucer	$1-2
10" plate	$6-8
8" plate	$5-7
6" plate	$1-2
Coupe soup	$4-6
Lug soup	$6-8
Fruit cup	$1-2
11" platter	$7-9
13" platter	$8-10
Medium nappy	$8-10
Large nappy	$7-9
Baker	$7-9
Sugar	$7-9
Creamer	$3-4
Tall creamer	$10-12
Handled soups	
French casseroles	$10-12
Cake Plate, Laurel shape	$8-10
Teapot	$20-25
Coffeepot	$18-20
Shakers, pair	$6-8
Sauceboat	$7-9
Casserole	$12-15
Pickle	$7-9
Covered butter	$10-12
Divided baker	$7-9
Chop plate	$8-10

Vistosa

Tea cup	$12-15
Tea saucer	$3-4
10" plate	$45-50
9" plate	$15-20
7" plate	$10-12
6" plate	$8-10
Coupe soup	$18-20
Lug soup	$20-25
5" fruit cup	$8-10
8 ½" nappy	$40-45
12" chop platter	$35-40
15" chop platter	$55-60
Creamer	$15-20
Sugar	$25-30
Teapot	$125+
Footed salads:	
ruffled foot	$250+
plain foot	$200-225
Water jug	$85-110
Sauceboat	$250+
Shakers, pair	$15-20
Egg cup	$45-50
AD coffee cup	$30-35
AD coffee saucer	$12-15

Vogue

10" plate	$8-10
9" plate	$6-8

8" plate, round	$8-10	Teapot	$35-40	6"	$3-4
8" plate, square	$8-10	AD cup	$10-12	Bread tray	$6-8
7" plate	$4-6	AD saucer	$2-3	Handled tray	$6-8
6" plate	$2-3	Creamer	$3-4	Teacup	$4-6
Teacup	$4-6	Sugar, covered	$7-9	Tea saucer	$1-2
Saucer	$1-2	Covered casserole	$18-20	Creamer	$3-4
15" platter	$15-18	Sauceboat	$8-10	Sugar, covered	$7-9
13" platter	$10-12	36s bowl	$8-10	Covered casserole	$12-15
11" platter	$10-12	Pickle/sauce-		Sauceboat	$8-10
9" platter	$7-9	boat liner	$6-7	5" Fruit cup	$1-2
Sauceboat	$8-10	Round platters:		6" Oatmeal	$2-3
Gravy fast-stand	$10-12	13"	$8-10	Rim soup	$4-6
Covered casserole	$20-25	11"	$6-8	Lug soup	$4-6
Sugar	$8-10	10"	$6-8	Nappy	$5-7
Creamer,		5" Fruit cup	$1-2	Oval baker	$5-7
regular opening	$6-8	6" Oatmeal	$2-3	Shakers, pair	$8-12
Lug soup	$6-8	Coupe soup	$4-6	36s bowl	$8-10
Fruit cup	$2-3	Lug soup	$4-6		
Oatmeal bowl	$4-6	Vegetable bowls:			
36s bowl	$10-12	7 ¾"	$5-7		

Kitchenware

Soup	$7-9
Baker, any size	$7-9
Nappy, any size	$7-9
Lug cake plates:	
with rim	$7-9
without rim	$10-12

9 1/8"	$5-7
Covered butter dish	$10-12
Coffee mug	$15-18
Double eggcup	$10-12
Tumbler	$20-25
Coaster	$10-15
Jug	$20-25
Coffeepots:	
64-oz.	$35-40

Tilt-top jug	$20-25
6-cup teapot	$20-25
Open jug	$12-15
Covered casserole	$12-15
Mixing bowls, ea.	$10-12
Drip jar with lid	$10-12
Range shakers	$8-10
Salad bowl	$10-12
Fork	$15-18

Covered butter	$20-25
Teapot	$30-35

36-oz.	$35-40
Shakers, pr.	$6-8
Tid-bit	$18-20

Spoon	$15-18
Pie server	$10-12
4" leftover	$8-10
5" leftover	$10-12
6" leftover	$15-18
Handled mug	$8-10
Ramekin	$3-5
Small bean pot	$3-5
Pie plate	$8-10

Ballerina

Plates:	
10"	$6-8
9"	$5-7
7"	$4-6
6"	$3-4
Square	$6-8
Teacup	$4-6
Tea saucer	$1-2

Camwood Ivory, Laurella, Rodeo, Sunrise

Plates:	
10"	$6-8
9"	$5-7
7"	$4-6